W9-BVJ-440

199

THE NATIONAL COUNCIL OF TEACHERS OF ENGLISH

ENGLISH MONOGRAPH NO. 16

TEACHING ENGLISH USAGE

TEACHING ENGLISH USAGE

by

ROBERT C. POOLEY

Professor of English, University of Wisconsin

TEXAS SOUTHMOST COLLEGE LIBRARY
1825 MAY STREET, FT. BROWN
BROWNSVILLE, TEXAS 78520

APPLETON-CENTURY-CROFTS, INC.

NEW YORK

COPYRIGHT, 1946, BY

THE NATIONAL COUNCIL OF TEACHERS OF ENGLISH

All rights reserved. This book, or parts thereof, must not be reproduced in any form without permission of the publisher.

439

PRINTED IN THE UNITED STATES OF AMERICA

Preface

This book is the product of twenty years of reading, teaching, and writing in the fascinating area of English usage. A considerable part of the content has appeared earlier in professional journals, or in pamphlets or books now out of print. Chapters I and II were written for *English Usage: A Teaching Problem,* a pamphlet publication of the Wisconsin English Teachers' Association released in 1934. Chapter III appeared first in *Educational Method* for March, 1937. Chapter IV was published as an article in the *English Journal* for January, 1945, at the request of the editor. Chapters VI, VII, and VIII are adapted from *Grammar and Usage in Textbooks on English,* Bureau of Educational Research Bulletin No. 14, August, 1933. Grateful acknowledgment is made to the editors and publishers concerned for permission to reprint the materials here. Other specific acknowledgments are made in footnotes.

In a work of this kind practically every paragraph is shaped by the conscious or unconscious influence of a writer or teacher in the field of usage. To the hundred or more writers who are quoted the author expresses his deepest appreciation for their share in his task. For laying the foundations of his interest in English usage, the author expresses gratitude to the late Professor Sterling Andrus Leonard, to the late Professor William Ellery Leonard, to Professor E. A. Cross, and to Professor Miles

Hanley. For careful reading of the manuscript and for valuable suggestions toward its revision grateful thanks is expressed to Dr. Luella B. Cook of the Minneapolis Public Schools, to Professor Thomas F. Dunn of Drake University, to Professor James B. McMillan of the University of Alabama, and to Professor Fred G. Walcott of the University of Michigan.

R. C. P.

Acknowledgments

Grateful acknowledgment is made to the authors and publishers listed below for permission to reprint quotations.

George Allen and Unwin Ltd. for quotations from *Philosophy of Grammar* by Otto Jespersen.

American Book Company for quotations from *New Essentials of English* by H. C. Pearson and M. F. Kirchway.

D. Appleton-Century Company, Inc. for permission to reprint from *Growth and Structure of the English Language* by Otto Jespersen. Copyright, 1923, by D. Appleton and Company.

The Clarenden Press for permission to quote from *English Idioms* by Logan Pearsall Smith, Tract 12, Society for Pure English.

Professor C. C. Fries and Professor Bernard Bloch for permission to quote from the article "The Expression of the Future" in *Language,* Vol. 3, No. 2, June, 1927.

Harcourt, Brace and Company for permission to reprint selections from *Pupil Activity English Series,* Book 8, by T. J. Kirby and M. F. Carpenter.

D. C. Heath and Company for permission to quote selections from *Two Book Course in English* (1900) Book II, by Mary F. Hyde; and from *Syntax* by George O. Curme.

Henry Holt and Company for permission to quote from *The Knowledge of English* by George Philip Krapp.

Houghton Mifflin Company for permission to quote from *The Dance of Life* by Havelock Ellis.

Mrs. George Philip Krapp for permission to quote from *A Comprehensive Guide to Good English* by George Philip Krapp.

The Macmillan Company for permission to quote from *Composition for College Students,* by J. M. Thomas, F. A. Manchester, and F. W. Scott; from *Words and Their Ways in English Speech* by J. B. Greenough and G. L. Kittredge; from *Fundamentals in English* by E. A. Cross. By permission of The Macmillan Company, publishers.

Saturday Review of Literature for a quotation from "Educational Quackery" by S. A. Leonard.

Charles Scribner's Sons for quotations from *Modern English* by George Philip Krapp.

H. H. Setzler for permission to quote from "Is the Subjunctive Disappearing?" by E. B. Setzler.

Scott, Foresman and Company for quotations from *English Usage* by J. Lesslie Hall.

University of Wisconsin Press for permission to quote from *The Doctrine of Correctness in English Usage* by S. A. Leonard.

Warwick and York, Inc. for quotations from "The Dangling Participle Due" by J. K. Kenyon, *American Speech,* Vol. 6, October, 1930.

Williams and Wilkins Company for quotations from "Shall and Will" by S. A. Leonard, *American Speech,* Vol. 4, August, 1929; "Conservatism in American Speech," George H. McKnight, *American Speech,* Vol. I, October, 1925; "On Usage in English" by Reuben Steinbach, *American Speech,* Vol. 4, December, 1928; "The Misrelated Constructions" by Reuben Steinbach, *American Speech,* Vol 5, December, 1929; "If for Whether" by A. J. Zieglschmid, *American Speech,* Vol. 5, October, 1929; "The Split Infinitive" by George O. Curme, *American Speech,* Vol. 2, May, 1927.

Contents

PART I

THE BACKGROUND OF CORRECT USAGE

PART II

THE FACTS ABOUT USAGE

PART III

PROCEDURES IN TEACHING USAGE

PART I

THE BACKGROUND
OF CORRECT USAGE

I

The Problem of Correctness

"The Bible is written in very poor English, isn't it?" remarked a grade-school child to his father, as they walked home from church.

"What makes you say that?" inquired the astonished parent, for whose ears the musical dignity of the King James Version approached the perfection of English prose.

"Well, our teacher said it was bad English to begin sentences with 'and.' But almost every sentence the minister read this morning began with 'and,'" replied the child.

The father smiled as he recognized the accuracy of the child's observation. The reading had been from the eighth chapter of the Gospel according to St. Matthew; it was true enough that almost every sentence began with "and." He thought a moment longer before he spoke. "Your teacher has made a natural mistake," he began. "In trying to give good advice to boys and girls just learning to write, she has made a rule about 'and.' The rule is too big. People who know how to write well use 'and' correctly and effectively at the beginning of sentences. On the other hand, boys and girls in school use 'and' too much. Your teacher's purpose in trying to help you was good, but the rule she stated is untrue."

In this trifling episode may be found the epitome of the problem of correctness in English. It lies in the recurrent conflict between rule and practice. Rules of usage are usually made to cover specific situations, to govern the use of language at a certain time for a certain purpose. Gradually, as the rule is taught and applied, the specific purpose for which it was created is forgotten, and the rule is applied universally, often in defiance of a language custom centuries old. Take, for example, the much taught but erroneous rule that "a sentence must not end with a preposition." Or, as one grammar is supposed to have stated it, "A preposition is a bad thing to end a sentence *with*." In certain types of formal, literary English the terminal preposition is considered undesirable because of the rhetorical looseness it gives to the style. Because certain formalists disliked the construction, the rule was created. It was repeated, copied, placed in school books. Teachers unaware of the reason behind the origin of the rule, taught that a sentence must *never* end with a preposition. Teachers are still teaching this rule. Yet English for centuries has been idiomatically and correctly expressed in such sentences as: "Where are you from?" "I didn't know whom to give it to," "John will go, but I don't expect to," "What city has he lived in?" To apply the rule to such sentences as these, which are characteristic of informal or colloquial English, is to make an absurdity of a caution. Many such absurdities have been created and are being perpetuated through honest but misguided zeal.

In contrast to an example of this type is the undisputed fact that many people use forms of English which are universally deplored by all who are sensitive to good English. He done it, we have went, them books, where was you? are defended as correct English by no one. Yet these faults and many similar ones appear with regrettable persistency in the speech and writing of high-school students. Obviously correct usage must be taught and taught thoroughly to break down bad habits and substitute acceptable language patterns. Right here we face the difficulty. Some forms of usage must be taught so thoroughly that bad habits of speech and writing are entirely eradicated. Other forms of usage are best left untaught, or if mentioned at all, should be presented as cautions for specific types of writing and speaking. It is the purpose of this book to show what items of usage need to be taught, and in what manner to most effectively improve patterns of speech and writing. A parallel purpose is to show what obsolete "rules" can be safely ignored, and why they can be ignored. Furthermore, the purpose is to describe and illustrate borderline cases, and to present the principles governing sound judgment in such cases.

Even more important than the analysis of specific items of usage is the development of a linguistically sound attitude toward problems of usage. One of the most perplexing problems of the English teacher today is to determine a valid and workable theory of correct English. It is obvious to any cultivated person that society demands certain standards in language usage, the observation of which marks a person of education and culture. It is equally obvious to the enlightened observers that many of the rules of the textbooks on grammar and guides to good English are in some instances only partially right and in others unquestionably wrong and misleading.

These discrepancies between rule and practice have led in recent times to two extreme attitudes, each unfortunate in its results. New attitudes toward usage, only partially understood, have led to perfectly understandable confusion. One group of teachers, made uneasy by the way in which revised ideas about correctness seem to tolerate all sorts of carelessness, feel that the remedy lies in a renewed emphasis on all the rules and a stiff course in grammar to support them. The other group, quite rightly finding some of the rules obsolete or invalid, tend to throw out all rules and even the teaching of all usage, feeling that no standard is better than a faulty standard. There is a middle ground, however, between purism and anarchy, upon which English teachers may safely stand in dealing with questions of usage. It is the over-all purpose of this book to point out the way to a sound and tenable theory of correctness in English usage, to resolve specific problems of usage in the light of this theory and to present practical classroom methods for instruction in usage all the way from the grossest errors of grammar to the subtle refinements of literary style.

II

Historical Backgrounds of English Usage

The English language in the Elizabethan period underwent an enormous expansion in its vocabulary. From travelers on the Continent and in the New World, from the scholars of the classical languages in the universities, and from experiments among English writers there poured in a flood of words, most of which became assimilated into the language. Part of the effervescence of the Elizabethan era found its vent in the game of words—not before or since has English witnessed such absorbing interest in words and their meanings, nor such an enormous increase in the number of words. Grammar, on the other hand, attracted little attention and was taken for granted. While the major outlines of English grammar had become fairly fixed by the time of Shakespeare and were essentially the grammar we know today, it was a popular or traditional, rather than a formal, grammar. A study of the usage of Elizabethan dramatists, for example, reveals far greater freedom in number agreement, in double comparatives, and in double negatives than is tolerated in current writing. Elizabethan dramatic literature, in short, is a faithful reproduction of the normal speech of Elizabethan gentlemen, who wrote as they spoke, unhampered by considerations of formal correctness.

The verbal enthusiasm of the Elizabethan era was followed by a natural reaction toward restraint. From the beginning of the seventeenth century there appeared a critical attitude toward English, voiced at first by a few scattered writers who felt that English was an uncouth and disorderly language, lacking the beauty and regularity of Latin and Greek. Gradually the idea of the impurity and irregularity of English came to be commonly accepted, so that by the end of the seventeenth century the interest in language had shifted almost entirely from vocabulary to grammar and syntax. This change of interest was accompanied by a zeal for reform and by a great increase in the numbers of books on the English language. Prior to 1700 there were few books devoted to language criticism; in the first half of the eighteenth century approximately fifty such books appeared, and in the succeeding half century over two hundred were published. These figures reveal the tremendous interest in language which characterized the latter part of the eighteenth century.

The same spirit which brought about the Augustan Age of English literature, the "improving" of Shakespeare and the editing of Milton, accelerated the purifying and correcting of English. That a large part of the critical work in English was beneficial to the language cannot be denied, but unfortunately there was much bad mixed with the good. Many of the writers on language were retired clergymen and country philosophers, who, though possessing some skill in the classics, had no conception at all of the history of English or the methods of linguistic research. Too frequently their statements on English usage were the product of false philology or of personal prejudice. Moreover, the philosophy of the age was inimical to scientific research in language; the prevailing conceptions of language were (1) that language is a divine institution, originally perfect, but debased by man; (2) that English is a corrupt and degenerate off-spring of Latin and Greek. The first theory gave rise to the application of reason and the analogy of the language in an effort to restore English to its pristine glory; the second resulted in corrections of English idioms to make them conform to classical models. The actual usage of English was ignored or despised by all but one or two of the writers of this age.

Thus we find the laudable effort to improve and correct the grammar and syntax of English sadly handi-capped by ignorance of linguistic principles on the one hand and misleading philosophies on the other. Yet the prescriptions of the reformers, whether good or bad, were received, approved, and formulated into rules; the rules were gathered into textbooks and were copied from book to book throughout the nineteenth century and may still be found in the books we are now using. In the meantime the English language has continued its organic growth, only slightly influenced by the rules prescribed for it, until today many of the rules bear no more than a faint resemblance to the language customs they are supposed to describe. It is small wonder that English teachers are perplexed in trying to reconcile dead rules with a living language!

The links between the reformers of the eighteenth century and the textbooks of today may be easily traced. One of the most influential of the eighteenth-century writers on language was Bishop Lowth, whose *Short Introduction to English Grammar* appeared in 1762. In 1795 an American named Lindley Murray wrote a grammar, nearly all of which he copied from Lowth. Murray's book enjoyed an enormous popularity; it is estimated that over a million copies were sold in America before 1850. Murray's successors copied freely from his book, so that the direct influence of Lowth persisted well into the latter part of the nineteenth century. The vast expansion of the United States since the Civil War, the accompanying increase in the numbers of textbooks, and the greatly improved theories and methods of education have resulted in textbooks very different in character from those of Lowth and Murray; but whereas in organization and technique the books have made great forward strides, in actual content they still retain much of the theory and practice of the eighteenth and nineteenth centuries.

The teaching of English usage is still further confused by the conflict between the traditional rules, whose origins we have just traced, and the modern science of linguistics, which is giving us entirely new concepts of language and its functions. Linguistics teaches us to look at language from the viewpoints of history, psychology, and sociology, and to understand and interpret modern usage in the light of these factors rather than upon a set of traditional authorities. Some examples of the application of these principles may be interesting to include here.

History. Many textbooks contain warnings against the use of the word *slow* as an adverb, pointing out that *slow* is an adjective with a corresponding adverb *slowly*. But when we look back into the history of English, we discover that adverbs were formed in two ways in early English; sometimes by adding *-lic* (the ancestor of *-ly*) and sometimes by just adding *-e*. Thus the descendant of *slow-lic* is *slowly*, a regular adverb, and the descendant of *slow-e* is *slow*, an irregular or "flat" adverb. Both are correct, native English; both have been used in English literature; and both may be used today. The decision as to when to use one or the other is a matter of euphony and appropriateness in the sentence; one need never hesitate to say, "Drive slow!"

Psychology. Textbooks warn us about placing *only* in the sentence so that it is next to the word it modifies; for example, a sentence like this would be called incorrect by many textbooks: "I *only* had five dollars." Logically it is incorrect, because *only* appears to modify the pronoun *I,* but psychologically it is correct, because custom has established the pattern of the sentence beyond possibility of misunderstanding. If you wanted to say that you were the only one to have five dollars, you would have to say, "I *alone* had five dollars," or "*Only* I had five dollars." The regular pattern, "I *only* had five dollars," has but one meaning, namely, that you possessed no more than five dollars. In this manner the psychology of sentence patterns supersedes logic.

Sociology. The only valid basis for the creation, preservation, or extinction of a word is its usefulness to society. If the people need a word it will live; if it is no longer needed it will die. For this reason the Old English word *a,* which meant *law,* was completely eradicated by the Scandinavian word *law* because the latter was less open to confusion, and therefore more useful to society. In similar fashion a modern need is establishing the foreign word *data* as a singular noun meaning *information* or *collection of facts,* despite the fact that it is a Latin plural. There is little doubt that a few more years will establish "The *data is* complete," not because of logical correctness, but because society finds the word

data useful as a singular noun. These are but a few of the
hundreds of examples which might be cited.

THE DETERMINATION OF "CORRECT" ENGLISH

In the year 1712 Dean Swift wrote a letter to the
Earl of Oxford outlining a plan for the foundation of an
English academy similar to the French Academy for the
purpose of regularizing and establishing correct English.
Although his plan was received with interest, it was
never acted upon, and many later attempts to found an
academy have failed. The purists of the later eighteenth
century did much of what Swift desired, but fortunately
for the life and vigor of our tongue it has never been
submitted to the restraint of a board of authorities.
Several theories of "correctness" in English have therefore been formulated and have influenced writers and
teachers of the past and present. One of the most important of these theories was that enunciated by George
Campbell in 1776, that "correctness" rests in good
custom, defined as "national," "reputable" and "present."
This definition was accepted by practically all the nineteenth-century grammarians (although they frequently
did it violence in specific instances), and may be found
in a number of the high-school composition books of the
present day. Another theory, really a modification of
Campbell's, proposed by Fitzedward Hall and other
nineteenth-century students of language, is that "good
usage is the usage of the best writers and speakers."
This definition is also very widely used in the textbooks
of today, and is probably the expressed or implied
standard of good English in almost every American
schoolroom. Both of these definitions, useful as they have
been and are, present many difficulties in application to
the teaching of current usage.

The chief difficulty lies in the interpretation of the terms "reputable" and "the best writers and speakers." For example, nearly all grammar books list as undesirable English the use of the split infinitive, the dangling participle or gerund, the possessive case of the noun with inanimate objects, the objective case of the noun with the gerund, the use of *whose* as a neuter relative pronoun, and many others; yet all of these uses may be found in the authors who form the very backbone of English literature and who are "reputable" and the "best writers" in every sense of the words. If the standard-makers defy the standards, to whom shall we turn for authority? Moreover, the use of literary models tends to ignore the canon of *present* usage, for by the time an author has come to be generally recognized as *standard* his usage is no longer *present*. And among present speakers, who are best? The writer has heard a large number of the most prominent platform speakers of the day, yet he has still to hear one who did not in some manner violate the rules of the books. Are all great writers and speakers at fault, or is it possible that the rules are inaccurate?

The way out of this perplexity is to shift the search for standards away from "authorities" and traditional rules to the language itself as it is spoken and written today. Just as the chemist draws his deductions from the results of laboratory experiments, the biologist from his observation of forms of life, and the astronomer from his telescope, so must students of language draw their deductions from an observation of the facts of language. In establishing the laws of language, our personal desires, preferences, and prejudices must give way to the scientific determination and interpretation of the facts of language. What language we use ourselves may take any form we desire, but the making of rules and the teaching of rules must rest upon objective facts. We must take the attitude of a distinguished scholar who said recently of *due to*, "I don't like it, but there is no doubt about its establishment in English."

If we discard the authority of rules and of "reputable" writers, to what can we turn for a definition of "correct" English? At the outset it must be acknowledged that there can be no absolute, positive definition. "Correct English" is an approximate term used to describe a series of evaluations of usage dependent upon appropriateness, locality, social level, purpose, and other variables. It is a relative term, in decided contrast with the positive nature of (1) *reputability*, the determination of good usage by reference to standard authors; (2) *preservation*, the obligation to defend and maintain language uses because they are traditional, or are felt to be more elegant; (3) *literary*, the identification of good usage with formal literary usage. By discarding these traditional conceptions, and turning to the language itself as its own standard of good usage, we may find the following definition adequate for our present needs. *Good English is that form of speech which is appropriate to the purpose of the speaker, true to the language as it is, and comfortable to speaker and listener. It is the product of custom, neither cramped by rule nor freed from all restraint; it is never fixed, but changes with the organic life of the language.*

Such a definition is linguistically sound because it recognizes the living, organic nature of language; it is historically sound, for the language of the present is seen to be the product of established custom; it is socially sound in recognizing the purpose of language and its social acceptability in *comfort* to speaker and writer.

Teachers of English will recognize that the acceptance of this or a similar definition of good English necessitates great changes in the presentation of usage in textbooks and in the classroom. Those who are accustomed to rule and authority, to an absolute right and wrong in language, will find great difficulty in making the mental readjustment imperative for a relative rather than an absolute standard of usage. Much of the conventional teaching of grammar and correctness will have to be vastly modified or discarded. There will be much confusion and some distress. But eventually there will grow up in the schools a new theory of good English so closely knit with the language itself that the perplexity now arising from the discrepancies between rule and usage will no longer have cause for existence. But in discarding an absolute right and wrong for a relative standard of appropriateness and social acceptability, we shall have to determine the areas or levels of language usage, to define and illustrate them, and to apply them as standards for the written and spoken English in the schools. Such an attempt is presented in the next chapter.

III

Levels in English Usage

It is obvious that when such terms as *appropriate,*
customary, comfortable, or *socially desirable* are used in
defining the nature of good English usage, the conception of a single standard or level of correctness can no
longer prevail. Speech is a form of human behavior, and
like all forms of human behavior, is subject to almost
infinite variety. But in even the most primitive societies
human behavior is made subject to certain restraints,
determined and maintained by the social group. Some of
these are fundamental, essential to the life of the group,
like the prohibition of murder; others are ceremonial in
character, applying to all members of the group at
certain times, or to some members of the group at all
times. In somewhat similar fashion language usages are
subjected to the restraints of society. At all times those
who speak a language are required to keep within the
limits of intelligibility in order to be understood;
language which departs from custom so far as to be
incomprehensible defeats its own purpose. But in addition to fundamental understanding there are ceremonial
distinctions in language to be found in the most primitive
societies; the language of the council fire or religious
observance differs in vocabulary and tone from that of
the hunt or the harvest. In civilized societies the same
principle prevails, except that greater complexity of life
calls forth a wider range of differentiations in usage. It

will cause no surprise upon reflection to realize that we all more or less unconsciously distinguish three or more gradations or levels in our language usage; there is the informal intimate speech of the home and of our hours of recreation; the slightly restrained speech of semi-public occasions, like conversation with strangers; and the carefully chosen, deliberate language of public address on formal occasions. Each of these has its analogue in writing. Moreover, business and professional people are very apt to employ a technical vocabulary among their colleagues, sometimes almost incomprehensible to the uninitiated. It seems beyond doubt reasonable, therefore, that this differentiation of language usage, a fundamental law of language, should be our first consideration in the study of "correct" English and in the presentation of English usage in the classroom. The purpose of this chapter is to define and illustrate the levels of English usage and to point out their relative values in the social group.

THE ILLITERATE LEVEL

The words and phrases typical of this level of English usage mark the user as belonging definitely outside the pale of cultivated, educated society. They have no standing whatever in literature, except in the dialect conversation of characters deliberately portrayed as illiterate or uncultivated. Although comparatively few in number, they are widespread and extremely common in the speech of the uneducated. They cannot be tolerated in the classroom except in deliberate attempts to reproduce the conversation of illiterate characters.

EXAMPLES

If I had *of* come, he wouldn't *of* done it.
I got the measles *off* Jimmie.

TEXAS SOUTHMOST COLLEGE LIBRARY
1825 MAY STREET, FT. BROWN
7025 BROWNSVILLE, TEXAS 78520

He *give* me the book. (past tense)

They *was,* we *was,* you *was*

I *is,* you *is,* they *is,* them *is*

He *came, done, seen, run,* etc.

Have went, have come, have did, have saw, have ran, have drank, etc.

The double negative, as in: *didn't have no, won't never, can't never, couldn't get no,* etc.

Them books

Youse

I *ain't,* you *ain't,* etc.

Growed, knowed, blowed, seed, etc.

That there, this here

He looked at me and *says*

Leave me do it.

He did *noble, good, swell,* etc.

THE HOMELY LEVEL

The words and phrases typical of this level are outside the limits of standard, cultivated usage, yet are not completely illiterate. They characterize the speech of many worthy men and women with some claim to literacy, who by the accident of birth, occupation, or geographical location are denied the society of more cultivated persons. The children in many of our rural schools come from homes in which the parents speak the English of this level. It behooves the teacher, therefore, to have an understanding sympathy for this type of speech, and while zealously seeking to build up in the children a dialect more closely approaching standard English, to refrain from ridiculing the speech of the home or from characterizing it unreservedly as "bad English." Tactful understanding will do far more than rigid purism in creating among these children a respect for the more standard forms of speech and a desire to attain a higher standard of usage.

EXAMPLES

He *don't* come here any more.
I *expect* you're hungry.
Stop the bus; I *want out*.
Mary's mother, *she* isn't very smart.
I *got* an apple right here in my hand.
I *haven't hardly* time.
We *can't scarcely* do it.
Just where are we *at*?
He *begun, sung, drunk, eat,* etc.
The various forms of confusion in *lie* and *lay*, *sit* and *set*,
   rise and *raise*
I *want for* you to do it.
The dessert was made with *whip cream*.
He comes *of a Sunday*.
John *was raised* in Kentucky.
This is *all the farther* we can go.
Calculate (or cal'late, reckon) for *guess, suppose*
A light-*complected* girl
Hadn't he ought to do it?

To this homely level of English speech belong also the
local dialect uses not generally recognized over the
United States, like the *to home* for *at home*, of New
England; the *admire* for *like* of the South; the *loco* for
crazy of the West; and the characteristic idioms of the
mountaineers in the Blue Ridge and Ozark ranges.

STANDARD ENGLISH, INFORMAL LEVEL

The range of standard English is necessarily very wide.
It must include all the words, phrases, forms, and idioms
employed by the great mass of English-speaking people
in the United States whose dialect lies between the
homely level and the decidedly literary level. It must be
wide enough to include the variations of language usage
common among people of education; the speech of the
home, of the hours of business and recreation, as well as

that of the party and formal reception. In written form it must include the most informal of personal correspondence to the formal phrasing of the business and social note. Standard English is, in fact, *the language;* it is present, ordinary, comfortable usage, with sufficient breadth in limits to permit of the shades of difference appropriate to specific occasions.

The informal level of standard English includes words and phrases commonly used by people of culture and education in their more informal moments, but which are generally excluded from formal public address, social conversation with strangers, and formal social correspondence. Informal standard English should be the normal usage of the teacher in the classroom and the goal which is set for the pupils to attain. A large part of the confusion arising from the teaching of usage in schools has been the result of trying to maintain the formal standard dialect, appropriate to careful writing, for the conversational needs of the schoolroom. There is no more need for children to be bookish in their schoolroom speech than for the teacher herself to be bookish in her intimate conversation.

The examples listed here for the informal standard level include only those items which may be employed informally but which are generally excluded from formal standard English.

EXAMPLES

He *blamed* the accident *on* me.
The *picnic* was a failure, *due to* a heavy shower.
No one knows what *transpires* in Washington.
Does anyone know *if* he *was* there?
I have never seen anyone act *like* he does.
His attack on my paper was most *aggravating.*
Most everyone is familiar with this picture
Where can you get *these kind* of gloves?

We had just two dollars *between* the four of us.
I *can't help but* go to the store.
Who did you send for?
John is the *quickest* of the two.
They were *very pleased* with the new house.
It was *good and cold* (*nice and warm*) in the room.
I *will try and do* it.
They invited John and *myself*.
Did you *get through with* your work?
As long as you have come, we can start.

STANDARD ENGLISH, FORMAL LEVEL

It is quite in accord with the customs of language usage that "correct" English have considerable variety in range of appropriateness, two levels of which are distinguished in this study by the terms *informal* and *formal* standard English. In general the leading characteristics of the more formal level of standard English are (1) greater restraint in vocabulary, with the avoidance of words distinctly informal in tone; (2) greater attention to formal agreement in number, both in subject-verb and pronoun-antecedent relationships, in tense sequence, and in case-agreement of pronouns; (3) greater attention to word order, particularly with respect to the position of modifying words, phrases, and clauses, and the use of a more complex sentence structure.

In the schoolroom this formal level of standard English should be the goal set for careful theme-writing, especially in what is commonly called the "thought theme," whether expository or argumentative. Narration and the various kinds of informal essays, as well as friendly letters, need not be held to the more exacting requirements of the formal standard level. It is, however, of great importance that children recognize the characteristics of both levels, and are able to use either appropriately.

To this level of English usage belong not only the public speech and formal writing of educated people, but also much of the printed material generally classed as "literature." Writing designed primarily for communication, as for example news articles, editorials, textbooks, and other expository compositions, unless distinctly technical or artistic in aim, employ the usages of the formal standard level.

It is rather difficult to offer many distinctive examples of formal standard usage, inasmuch as it is characterized by a general tone of restraint and care more than by the use of certain expressions. A few examples, however, may be found which are quite typical of the formal standard level.

EXAMPLES

I *shall* be glad to help you.
Neither of the party *was* injured.
Here are three *whom* we have omitted from the list.
I *had rather* stay at home.
We *had* better complete this investigation.
Under the circumstances, he did as well as might be expected.
The use of connectives like *furthermore, notwithstanding, despite, inasmuch as, on the contrary*

THE LITERARY LEVEL

It must be granted at the outset that the definition of the literary level of English usage employed in this study is somewhat arbitrary, and is more narrow in scope than the definitions of many textbooks. But since much of the difficulty in the teaching of English usage centers about the confusion of the terms *literary, standard,* and *correct* English, a most earnest attempt has been made in this book to differentiate the terms and to clarify their meanings and applications. It is therefore assumed that what is commonly called "correct" English includes the usages of at least three levels: the informal standard, the formal standard, and the literary levels, the correctness of any specific item in any given instance being dependent upon its appropriateness. The first two levels have been defined; it remains to describe the third.

Literary English is taken to mean that form of speech or writing which in aim goes beyond mere utility to achieve beauty. It differs from formal standard English not so much in kind as in purpose and effect. In diction it seeks not only accuracy in meaning but also a subjective quality of suggestion aroused by the sound of the word or the associated ideas and feelings. In form it goes beyond mere orderliness to achieve rhythm, symmetry, and balance. In every respect it surpasses the ordinary prose of communication in the attainment of aesthetic values transcending the needs of everyday expression.

An illustration of the difference between standard formal English and literary English may be seen in the opening sentence of Lincoln's "Gettysburg Address." Had Lincoln said, "Eighty-seven years ago our ancestors established on this continent a new nation, inspired by the spirit of liberty, and actuated by the theory that all men are created equal," he would have met adequately the demands of clear, formal communication. But in his phrasing, "Four score and seven years ago, our fathers brought forth on this continent a new nation, conceived in liberty, and dedicated to the proposition that all men are created equal," there are to be found those characteristics of the literary style which transcend communication. The literary tone of *fourscore and seven, fathers, dedicated to the proposition* is at once apparent; the associations awakened by the words *brought forth, conceived,* and *dedicated* give them emotional depths unsounded by *established, inspired,* or *actuated;* moreover, the sentence as a whole moves with an effect of solemnity achieved only by the happy arrangement of accents and the sonorous quality of the vowels employed. These qualities combine to make this sentence artistic, literary prose of the highest order.

It is obvious that the literary level cannot be made a requirement for all students in schoolroom composition. It is too much the product of mental maturity and highly developed skill to be attainable by the average student, or indeed, by the average teacher. Therefore, while examples of beautiful prose should be given to pupils to study, and the few who are gifted should be encouraged to strive toward the development of a literary tone and style, the great body of school children should be expected to do no more than to cultivate the clear, direct English of communication, together with a feeling for the appropriateness of word and idiom to the purpose intended. Students in whom these perceptions have been engendered will always use "correct," adequate English.

IV

The Nature of Communication

Languages evolved in the history of man's development as the means by which an individual can convey information, thoughts, and ideas to one or many of his associates, and also as the means by which he can in turn receive information, thoughts, and ideas from others. Thus the nature of language is strictly functional and its purpose is to promote communication. Whatever forms of language facilitate clear, concise, and accurate communication may be defined as good language; whatever forms of language fail to communicate clearly, or lead to ambiguity and obscurity may, for practical purposes, be defined as bad language. This is an important principle whose significance will be developed in this chapter.

Communication occurs when a meaningful signal passes from a sender, who originates it, to a receiver, who understands it. In ordinary communication the sender transmits his message by signs, by speech, or by writing. To accomplish his end, the sender must have, of necessity, something to communicate and a medium of transmission. The medium is, for all but the most elementary types of communication, spoken and written language. The sender becomes increasingly effective as he develops through experience new material to communicate and advances his skill in the use of the medium. The receiver, too, must be responsive to the means of communication; he develops as he increases his powers to recognize and interpret the signals which come to him through the medium of language.

In communication, therefore, there are two elements always present—the material to be communicated and the medium (usually language) by which it is transmitted. It is a peculiar fallacy of language teaching in American schools and colleges that in teaching the use of language enormous stress is laid on the language itself, which is only the medium, to the great neglect of the material to be communicated, which after all is the more essential part of the communication. In the typical English classroom countless hours are spent on the analysis and classification of language forms, with drill and practice in their use, *in isolation from the specific needs of communication.* The number of moments given to the analysis and clarification of meaning in communication are all too few.

This overemphasis on language for its own sake is nowhere more clearly seen than in the common attitudes toward usage and in the teaching of correctness. Indeed, the primary force behind nearly all efforts to correct and "purify" the English language has been the distrust of change, the desire to conserve and perpetuate what is considered the tradition. The relationship of meaning to form or the relative clarity of two alternate forms, rarely enters discussions of usage. Yet our language is not a static medium, nor can it be made static. Words change, grammatical forms change, there are styles in syntax which vary from decade to decade. The teaching of English and correct usage must never lose sight of the fluid nature of language. Decisions in usage must be reached in terms of the efficiency of communication rather than in terms of preserving what has been or "improving" the language by appeals to logic, reason, etymology, or any other factor not consistent with communication.

The common attitude toward English usage and correctness is that some forms of English are "right" and some forms are "wrong." Such decisions are made in the absolute and are applied indiscriminately to all linguistic situations. From this practice arises the absurdities which were referred to in Chapter I. Actually any English is "right" which enables the speaker or writer to communicate clearly, efficiently, and accurately what he wants to say. The usage decisions affecting his employment of language for any specific purpose must be arrived at in the light of the communication itself and its purposes, and not from any external, arbitrary standards. Thus the factors governing communication in each specific instance set the standards of correctness for that communication; usage conceived of in this light is relative rather than positive, fluid rather than static, psychological rather than logical. In teaching usage the emphasis will have to turn from the indoctrination of absolute rules to the development of sensitivity to and appreciation of the factors governing communication.

THE FACTORS INFLUENCING COMMUNICATION

In every situation calling for speech or writing there are three factors influencing the form of the communication, or in other words, determining the nature of the language usage. These factors are: (1) the meaning to be communicated; (2) the intention or purpose of the communication; and (3) the tone or effect desired in the communication.

First in importance is the matter to be conveyed,

which may be a warning, a fact, an observation, a decision, or a judgment. The communication may vary in complexity from a monosyllabic cry of warning or expression of momentary emotion, as in "ouch!" "ugh!" "quick!" to an elaborately constructed sequence of sentences as in a legal decision, a literary evaluation, or a philosophical argument. In every case, whether simple or involved, the motivating force for the communication is the need to convey an idea to someone else. Therefore, the first factor determining the choice of words and their order in any linguistic situation is the desire to convey meaning from oneself to another in the most efficient way.

But the transfer of meaning is only one factor in communication. The second controlling factor influencing usage is the intent or purpose of the communication. In the following examples note how the same fact is expressed in word usage voicing widely differing intentions: (1) Pick up your gloves! (2) Pardon me, I believe you have dropped your gloves. (3) You've shed your mittens, old dear. (4) Can't you go anywhere without leaving those gloves behind? In each of these sentences the same meaning is expressed—someone has dropped or left behind a pair of gloves. But the intention of the different speakers is made clear by the words they have chosen to call attention to the same fact. The first speaker assumes an attitude of responsibility toward the owner of the gloves and reveals a relationship permitting the use of the imperative mood. This speaker might be a parent, a husband or wife, or a close associate. The second speaker, although he refers to the same circumstance as the first, reveals an intention of conventionalized courtesy. His word choice is typical of a stranger addressing another over a trifling circumstance. The same words spoken by an intimate of the glove-dropper would convey in most circumstances an intention of irony or sarcasm. The third speaker reveals an intention of affectionate reminder or mild remonstrance. The fourth speaker, however, reveals by his choice of words both a relationship of intimacy and unconcealed irritation or annoyance. The intent of his speech is not only to call attention to the gloves but also to give voice to remonstrance and exasperation.

Closely related to the second factor, the intent of the communication, is the third, the tone of the communication. Tone may be defined as the appropriateness of the word choice to the meaning and intention of the speaker. In the four sentences listed above, three of the speakers used the word *gloves* while the other substituted *mittens*. The tone of the third speaker was clearly playful and affectionate. Therefore, the word *mittens,* suggesting little gloves as an affectionate diminutive, was appropriate to the intention and set the desired tone.

There are clearly recognized gradations of tone in the expression of any idea. Take for example the commonplace circumstance of going to bed. At least five gradations of tone may be employed in expressing this idea, each one appropriate to a particular situation.

1. I think I'll hit the hay.
2. It's time for me to turn in.
3. I believe I'll go to bed.
4. I think it is time to retire.
5. I shall withdraw to seek repose.

What tone is conveyed by each of these usages to express the same meaning? Sentence 1. is intentionally slangy, appropriate only to intimate circumstances when humor is the intent. Sentence 2. is still intimate, but less slangy; it would pass as appropriate usage in the close family circle. Sentence 3. is the simplest and most direct of the five forms; it is acceptable usage in almost any circumstance. Sentence 4. implies less intimate circumstances; the word *retire* is a polite substitute for the blunt "go to bed." This form would be appropriate to a guest in the home of relative strangers. Sentence 5. is stilted and artificial. The simple act of going to bed makes such elaborate wording slightly ridiculous. Yet there are people with a mistaken idea of elegance who would approve sentence 5.

Almost innumerable examples of such gradations of tone can be found. As another example, consider the idea expressed by the verb *to go*.

1. You'd better scram!
2. Get out fast!
3. You ought to go.
4. It is necessary to depart.
5. Get thee hence!

IMPLICATIONS FOR TEACHING USAGE

It is hoped that three significant principles regarding English usage have emerged from this chapter. These principles are: (1) the correct usage of contemporary English cannot be determined by appeals to logic, etymology, or the traditions of former days. It cannot be determined by rules of "right" and "wrong." It must be determined by the needs of communication in every situation in which language is used.

(2) Since correctness is a relative matter, derived from the needs of communication, the teaching of correct English requires the development of sensitivity to the factors influencing communication: meaning, intention, and tone. Attention to these factors develops the art of

appropriateness in language, which is the foundation of correct usage.

(3) The teaching of correctness in school and college courses must shift in emphasis from the laying down of negative rules to the development of positive insights. The correction of errors is less than half the teaching of good usage. Far more important is the awakening in pupils' minds of a recognition of the nature of communication, a recognition of how communication determines usage, and the development of a sensitivity to the gradations of intent and tone in every communication created by the selection of appropriate words, idioms, and constructions. Exercises for the teaching of these skills are presented in Chapter XI.

PART II

THE FACTS ABOUT USAGE

V

The Sources of Usage Information

There is an extensive bibliography of materials dealing with the standards of correctness in English usage.[1] A sample list of this material is presented in the bibliography at the end of this book. Unfortunately a great deal of the material is available only to those who have access to a very large library, since much of it is in the form of articles in scholarly journals of small circulation or in pamphlets and monographs with a limited distribution. The classroom teacher, however, need not be greatly handicapped on this account, as the best part of these materials have been summarized and interpreted in the books described below, and to some extent in Chapters VI, VII, and VIII of this book. The purpose of this chapter is to describe and evaluate a few books which are easily obtainable, and which the professionally minded teacher may desire to add to his personal library.

BOOKS DEALING WITH ENGLISH USAGE

The books presented here are arranged in order of their dates of publication. The study of English usage as it affects the teaching of English is of fairly recent origin, the greater part of the materials having appeared in the last two decades. For the teacher who desires to follow

[1] See Arthur G. Kennedy, *A Concise Bibliography for Students of English* (Stanford University, Calif., Stanford University Press, 1940).

the progress of usage information in chronological order the following list will serve as an introduction. On the other hand, for general knowledge of usage problems and their proposed solutions any of the following books may be consulted without reference to publication dates.

1. HALL, J. Lesslie, *English Usage* (Chicago, Scott, Foresman and Company, 1917), 339 pp.

This book is both instructive and amusing. Taking up one by one a considerable list of questioned or disputed usages, the author presents the history of each item, a summary of the leading opinions on it, and extensive quotations from standard authors to illustrate the use of the item. *English Usage* has been quoted extensively in the following chapters of this book.

2. LEONARD, Sterling A., *Doctrine of Correctness in English Usage, 1700-1800,* University of Wisconsin Studies in Language and Literature, No. 25 (Madison, Wis., University of Wisconsin, 1929), 361 pp.

Professor Leonard laid the foundations for contemporary usage study in this book. He makes an intensive study of language attitudes in the eighteenth century, the period in which efforts to "correct" and "purify" English reached their highest degree. Tracing many so-called "rules" of correct English to their source, he shows that a large majority of the rules are founded on well-meaning but mistaken efforts to "correct" English on false concepts of language, on analogies with Latin and Greek, or on pure prejudice, some of it spiteful. While not all the contents are directly applicable to current problems, the book is rewarding for the light it throws on the sources of surviving misconceptions and prejudices.

3. LEONARD, Sterling A., *Current English Usage,* English Monograph No. 1 of the National Council of Teachers of English (Chicago, National Council of Teachers of English, 1932), 232 pp.

This study is the first attempt of any magnitude to secure contemporary opinions on disputed usage by direct appeal to qualified judges. Professor Leonard sent out a sheet containing 230 items of disputed usage placed in sentences and asked for the rating of each item by the judges, who included teachers of English at college and high-school levels, publishers, newspaper and magazine editors, other professional workers, and a group of business men. From the returns of this questionnaire the author attempted to prepare a table of acceptability of usage from the indisputably correct to the unquestionably incorrect. While some exceptions may be taken to both method and results, the study is nevertheless one of the milestones of usage interpretation and is worthy of every teacher's attention. The book contains also a study of punctuation based on ratings of typical punctuation uses by authors, editors, publishers, and so forth.

4. POOLEY, Robert C., "Grammar and Usage in Textbooks on English," Bulletin No. 14 (Madison, Wis., University of Wisconsin Bureau of Educational Research, 1933), 172 pp.

This study is based on an analysis of twelve composition textbook series in popular use from 1920-1930 at the elementary, high-school, and college levels. The author attempts to show the survival of eighteenth- and nineteenth-century misconceptions and prejudices regarding English usage in textbooks then contemporary. This study is out of print and is available only in libraries. It is listed here partly to complete the chronological picture of usage studies, and partly because it is the source of the specific usage materials presented in Chapters VI, VII, and VIII of this book, which in effect supersedes *Grammar and Usage in Textbooks on English*.

5. MARCKWARDT, Albert H., and WALCOTT, Fred G., *Facts About Current English Usage*, English Monograph No. 7 of the National Council of Teachers of English (New York, D. Appleton-Century Company, Inc., 1938), 144 pp.

Facts About Current English Usage is a successor to *Current English Usage*, listed as 3. above. Taking the view that the Leonard study was based on the opinions of judges, this monograph proposes to present the *facts* regarding the same usage items, drawing principally upon the *New English Dictionary* for the historical evidence. The conclusions of this study, however, must be considered as the opinions of the authors.

6. PERRIN, Porter G., *An Index to English* (Chicago, Scott, Foresman and Company, 1939), 680 pp.

Published as a college handbook for composition, this text is the first of the handbooks to take an objective and realistic approach to English usage problems. In alphabetical order it presents matters of usage, diction, grammar, and rhetoric as a guide to the writer and teacher of composition. It remains the most comprehensive and sound popular reference book. More recent editions, under the title, *Writer's Guide and Index to English,* place the material on language and rhetoric in the first half of the book, and the alphabetical index to grammar and usage in the latter half.

7. FRIES, Charles C., *American English Grammar,* English Monograph No. 10 of the National Council of Teachers of English (New York, D. Appleton-Century Company, Inc., 1940), 313 pp.

This is a pioneer book in the objective presentation of English grammar. Based on the assumption that grammar must be determined from the language as it is spoken and written today in the United States of America, it presents a true picture of modern American English without rules, definitions, or prescriptive statements of usage. It is rich in illustrations of the idiom of English in the United States.

8. KENNEDY, Arthur G., *English Usage* (New York, D. Appleton-Century Company, Inc., 1942), 166 pp.

Published under the auspices of the National Council of Teachers of English, *English Usage* is a guide to attitudes, materials, and decisions in the scientific study of usage prepared from the particular point of view of the teacher of English. It is not in itself a handbook of usage, but is rather an introduction to and an interpretation of the sources of information available to teachers. For the teacher who desires a concise statement of the linguistic point of view, with suggestions for the application of this point of view to the teaching of English, the book is excellent. It contains a well-selected bibliography for more extended reading.

9. KAULFERS, Walter V., *Four Studies in Teaching Grammar* (Stanford University, Calif. Stanford Bookstore, 1945), 47 pp.

Though not strictly a study in usage, this little monograph offers a significant point of view for teachers of language on the relationship between the grammar of a language and the use of a language. Study No. 2, "On the Teaching of English Grammar in the Elementary Grades and Junior High Schools" is particularly recommended.

PERIODICAL SOURCES

1. The most available current discussion of usage problems appears in the department labeled "Current English Forum," a monthly feature of *The English Journal* and *College English*. These journals go to members of the National Council of Teachers of English of high-school and college sections respectively. For information address the National Council of Teachers of English, 211 W. 68th Street, Chicago 21, Illinois.

2. Occasional articles on the teaching of usage appear in *The Elementary English Review*, a journal going to elementary-school section members of the National Council of Teachers of English.

3. Observations on current usages, articles evaluating usage questions, and reviews of books dealing with usage appear frequently in the journal, *American Speech*, which is published by the Columbia University Press, 2960 Broadway, New York, N. Y. A large number of the significant articles on English usage found in any comprehensive bibliography were published originally in *American Speech*.

OTHER SOURCES

1. *Dictionaries*. It is inevitable that the authors of dictionaries of English make some classification of the uses of words as a guide to the uses. Therefore such terms as *literary, technical, colloquial, slang, obsolete, archaic,* will be found in connection with certain words in most dictionaries. Two particular cautions should be observed in relying on dictionaries for the determination of usage:

   (*a*) Dictionaries are conservative and traditional in the handling of usage. Until an item has become well recognized on a national basis as acceptable usage, the dictionary tends to withhold approbation. Consequently, the usage labels given particular words or idioms in dictionaries should be taken as indices of usage, but not as authoritative pronouncements.

   (*b*) Except in rare cases, dictionaries deal with single words out of context rather than with words in phrases and sentences. Usage, on the other hand, is determined chiefly by the effect of a word or idiom *in context*. Dictionaries can rarely give counsel on when and how to use *stag* (meaning an unaccompanied gentlemen), *date* (meaning an engagement, the making of an engagement, or the person with whom one makes an engagement), *fix* (meaning a difficulty) and hundreds of other words and phrases which are appropriate to certain settings and inappropriate in others. Decisions in usages of this kind can seldom be made from dictionary classifications.

2. *Handbooks, desk manuals, etc.* The majority of publications claiming to be guides to correct usage must be consulted with caution. For the most part they present traditional and arbitrary decisions in usage derived from the "right-wrong" theories of the nineteenth century. They tend to ignore the changes which occur in usage from decade to decade, and they make no allowance for the degree of appropriateness of many usages in specific situations. One student wrote, "the sun *sits* at seven o'clock" because he had been advised by a handbook that *set* may never be used as an intransitive verb.

3. *Articles in newspapers and popular magazines.* Since these articles are derived largely from the handbooks and manuals mentioned above, the same caution in using them as authorities should be observed. The writer has observed in a popular metropolitan newspaper a brief article on the use of *none* with a singular verb stating a rule which was violated, and properly violated, in news columns of the same issue of the paper.

THE COMMUNITY AS A SOURCE

The best source of usage information is the community in which each individual lives. The community is the laboratory for the objective observation of English as it is actually used by all kinds of people. The alert teacher and pupil will discover in the community not one kind of English but many different kinds, each kind merging into the other. Further observation will reveal that these kinds of English may be roughly grouped into levels of language use, like those described in Chapter III of this book. These observations should be made in the spirit of scientific detachment to determine the actual facts of language usage in the community.

When the facts are determined with sufficient range to assure the validity of the observations, the data can be analyzed in somewhat the following manner:

1. What persons in the community appear to speak consistently the most approved forms of English?
   a. What positions do they hold in the community?
   b. What advantages of education, travel, and reading have they had?
   c. What particular characteristics of their speech produce the effect of superiority over the general dialect (common speech) of the community?
2. What persons in the community speak consistently a form of speech characterized by undesirable usages?
   a. What positions do they hold in the community?
   b. In what ways have circumstances limited their opportunities in education, travel, and reading?
   c. What particular characteristics of their speech produce the effect of inferiority to the general dialect (common speech) of the community?
3. What are the characteristics of the general dialect (common speech) of the community?
   a. Applying the definitions of levels of usage in Chapter III to the general dialect, what seems to be the level common to the community?
   b. What expressions consistently used in the local general dialect are sub-standard or illiterate? What expressions are typical of the homely level?
   c. What expressions or usages are strictly local or regional (common in this and neighboring communities, but not common to the United States)?
4. To bring the dialect of this community into harmony with the generally accepted usage level of spoken English in the United States, what particular steps must be taken?

a. Which usages of the sub-standard or illiterate level occur with greatest frequency?

b. Which expressions of the homely level are allowable in conversation? Which expressions of this level should be avoided in public conversation, as in school?

c. What idioms or usages, regional or local in character, is it desirable to retain in order to preserve a distinct individuality of speech?

An analysis of the speech of a community when undertaken by an individual or by a teacher and class together can be the most profitable activity in language study it is possible to find. The observers complete the investigation not only with substantial facts and the means of interpreting them, but with an entirely new concept of the nature of language, the varieties of its use, the absurdities of many rules, and an appreciation of the *social* rather than the *grammatical* basis for the determination of good language use.

VI

Problems in English Grammar

The materials dealt with in this chapter constitute items of actual morphology, (forms of words) distinguished from syntax, which is discussed in Chapter VII, and miscellaneous usage, presented in Chapter VIII. It is exceedingly difficult in a language as analytic as English to determine exactly where structure ends and syntax begins, and for that reason the basis of selection for items in this chapter is somewhat arbitrary. Only those grammatical matters which seem necessarily a part of a formal presentation of the English grammatical system find a place in this section. For example, the use of *shall* and *will* in a particular sentence may appear at first glance to be a question of syntax, but when it is recalled that nearly all complete grammar books present the paradigm of the simple future tense as:

> I shall (sing)
> thou wilt (sing)
> he will (sing)
> we shall (sing)
> you will (sing)
> they will (sing)

with no alternative forms except the more common second singular "you will sing," then the use of *will* as a first-person auxiliary becomes definitely a matter of morphology. On the other hand, the use of *so* as an intensifying adverb in no way alters the grammatical category of the word but simply involves word order in the sentence, and is rightly considered a problem of syntax.

As may be conjectured from the arbitrary use of the word *grammar* in this chapter, the parts of speech most affected are those of major importance in speech and writing; namely, the verb, the adverb, the noun, and the pronoun. Such problems as arise in connection with the other parts of speech (since, with the exception of the adjective, they are not inflected) are matters of syntax or usage, and are treated in appropriate chapters.

THE VERB

Present tense. Grammar books regularly list the present tense, active voice, indicative mode of the verb as follows:

> I sing
> you sing
> he sings
> we sing
> you sing
> they sing

No mention is made in any text of the fact that these forms as listed do not represent the ordinary present tense of actual usage, but rather constitute a sort of potential or habitual predication from which the element of time is almost entirely lost. "I sing" is equivalent to saying, "I am able to sing," or "I usually sing." The regular and common present-tense form to express action in the present is "I am singing." If a parent should inquire what his son was doing at the moment with the question, "What is Tommy doing?" the answer, "He plays" would be so unusual as to excite comment. "He is playing" is without doubt the expected answer. Textbooks and formal grammars have not accepted this common usage at all, still naming the form in -*ing* with the present tense of the verb *to be* as the present progressive, a conventional name with little or no real meaning. As a matter of fact the expression "I am singing" may be either a statement of immediate action, or a clear future, as in the sentence, "I am singing there tomorrow." Less frequently it is also used as a timeless or continuing present tense.

The timeless quality of the simple present-tense forms is readily recognized from a different angle, nevertheless, as the following quotations illustrate:

General truths and present facts should be expressed in the present tense, whatever the tense of the principal verb may be.[1]

Universal truths, or general propositions into which time relations do not enter, should usually be expressed in the present tense.[2]

The second statement is tempered with the word "usually" inspired no doubt by a realization of the fact that universal truths are not invariably expressed in the present tense. "If for such statements the present tense is generally used, it is in order to affirm that they are valid now. But other tenses may occasionally be used: We have the so-called 'gnomic preterit' as in Shakespeare's 'Men were deceivers ever'—what has hitherto been true, is so still and will remain so to the end of time."[3]

In unstudied speech the feeling for agreement in tenses seems to overbalance the feeling for the timelessness of the present tense in expressing general truths. Hence when one says, "I knew that Washington was the capital of the United States" there is no time quality felt in the word *was* since the word *knew* receives all the stress. In

[1] Brooks, p. 270.
[2] Raymond, p. 203
[3] Jespersen, *Philosophy of Grammar*, p. 259; see also p. 54.

its unaccented form it constitutes what Professor Jespersen calls the "gnomic preterit," meaning that "what has hitherto been true is so still and will remain so to the end of time," or at least for an indefinite period. The statement concerning the expression of general truths might well be, therefore, present facts and general truths as frequently expressed in the present tense because it is felt to be timeless. The past tense is also sometimes used, in agreement with a preceding past tense, when the idea of time is entirely absent from the second verb.

The school grammars of the future must distinguish clearly the uses of the present tense with time value and the uses without time value. Not until they do so will their treatment of the present tense be in accord with current usage.

Past tense. The textbooks quite generally list the usual past-tense forms of the verb, but none of them mention the following fairly common alternatives for expressing action habitual in the past: [4]

The participles *accustomed* and *wont* with the infinitive
The verb *used* with the infinitive
The auxiliary *would*

The forms might profitably be included in any discussion of predication in past time, for although they cannot be strictly classified as past-tense forms, they occupy an important place in ordinary speech.

In the inflection of irregular verbs, the leveled forms of the past tense, that is, those in more or less preponderant use at the present time, are generally listed without alternative, despite the not infrequent occurrence of "we sung," "the ship sunk," and others. One author, however,

[4] Lambert, p. 29.

perhaps with qualms of historical conscience, lists the
following alternative forms for the past tense: [5]

> began, begun
> shrank, shrunk
> sang, sung
> sank, sunk
> swam, swum

Another lists a single alternative form: [6]

> swung, or swang

That this particular verb should be singled out is especially astonishing in view of the fact that *swang* has
practically no history as a form and is strongly condemned by handbooks and guides to good usage.

Concerning these verbs the *New English Dictionary*
says:

> *sink*: The use of *sunk* as the p.t. has been extremely
> common. Johnson (1755) says "pret. I *sunk*,
> anciently *sank*."
>
> *sing*: *Sung* was the usual form of the p.t. in the
> 17th and 18th centuries, and is given by Smart in
> 1836 with the remark "Sang ... is less in use."
> Recent usage, however, has mainly been in favor
> of *sang*.
>
> *swing*: p.t. *swung*, rarely *swang*.
>
> *swim*: In Middle English p.t. sing. *swamme*; plur.
> *swummen*; standard p.t. *swam*.
>
> *shrink*: The p.t. originally had vowel change—*I
> shrank, we shrunke* (*n*), but as early as the 14th
> century the properly plural form is found with a
> singular subject and *shrank, shrunk* become fre-
> quent in the 15th century. *Shrunk* is the normal
> p.t. in the 18th century and still survives.

[5] Raymond, p. 218.
[6] Kirby and Carpenter, Book VII, p. 177.

> *begin*: As in other verbs having grammatical vowel
> change in the p.t. there was an early tendency to
> level the forms ... which has resulted in the estab-
> lishment of *began* as the standard form; but an
> alternative from the old plural *begun* has also
> come down to the present day.

The discussion of the word *drunk* in the *New English
Dictionary* is more full: "The past tense had originally
vowel change (I drank, we drunk) but leveled out to (I,
we drank). From the 16th to the 19th centuries *drunk* as
a past tense again appeared." This remark applies to
England and to some extent to colonial America. Later on
in the history of the United States the word *drunk* even
as a past participle became so objectionable that the past-
tense form *drank* was pressed into service. Today "have
drank" is old-fashioned rather than illiterate.

One of the textbook authors [7] lists the principal parts
of the verb *sink* as *sink, sank, sunk,* with no alternative in
the past tense. But on another page of the same text [8] occurs the quotation, "Down *sunk* the bell with a gurgling
sound." (Southey). Although the quotation is used here
as an illustration of an entirely different matter, the
bright-eyed student might well ask why Southey's grammar differs from that of the textbook. [9]

Contemporary textbooks may perhaps be forgiven for
the failure to note these alternative past-tense forms, but
there seems to be no justifiable reason for making issues
of them in exercises. It would seem advisable in presenting the past-tense forms of irregular verbs to give briefly

[7] Raymond, p. 127.

[8] *Ibid.,* p. 160.

[9] The form *sunk* is particularly interesting in this context because it is used as a singular. The past-tense forms in early Middle
English were: singular, *sank;* plural, *sunk.* In Southey's usage
the plural form had become preponderant; in our own day the
singular form is preferred.

and untechnically a little of their history, together with the alternate forms of the common verbs. The form now preponderant may be clearly indicated as a preferred form without doing violence to the history of the word.

Future tense. The future tense receives a good share of attention in contemporary textbooks since the authors no doubt feel that all contemporary speech usage and a fair amount of current writing usage is in direct violation of the traditional rules for the future. That the rules may be wrong and current usage right apparently has not occurred to the textbook writers. The following statements and rules are typical of the treatment of the future tense in the textbooks examined.[10]

Shall and *will* are used with the infinitive of a verb, to form the future tense. *Shall* is an auxiliary of the future in the first person, and *will* in the second and third persons.

To make a promise or to express the determination of the speaker, *will* is used in the first person and *shall* in the second and third persons.

In spite of the rules for the future tense, printed in traditional form in the heart of the text, one of the textbooks has for its first sentence, "We *will* begin our study of grammar and composition. . . ."[11]

Only one textbook breaks away entirely from the tradition and omits the future tense from all discussion. In a very modest section entitled "Tense" a brief discussion of the time values of verb forms is offered. The table subjoined presents examples of the various tenses, the future as follows:[12]

FUTURE: I will do, I will see, I will hear, I will know.

[10] Hyde, Book II, p. 131.
[11] McFadden and Ferguson, p. 1.
[12] Kirby and Carpenter, Book VIII, p. 312.

Not only is the future tense passed by as an item not worthy of discussion, but the very examples violate the rules of earlier textbooks. Can such rashness be justified? Compare now the statement of linguists and students of the historical aspects of language concerning the expression of the future.

1. Johannis Wallis, in his grammar of English (1615), written in Latin, was the first to state the rule for the use of *shall* in the first person, and *will* in the second and third persons. This discovery was made by Professor Fries.

    Whenever the subject of the verb is represented as in control of the situation, *will* is used in all three persons. *Shall* . . . is used in all three persons to represent that some other force, not the subject of the verb, is in control.

    Since *shall* is rather uncommon, it is, when stressed or emphasized, frequently heard in the first person for determination.[13]

2. The common school grammars of modern English usually give as the one means of indicating future time the combination of *shall* and *will* with the infinitive form of the verb and name it the "future tense." Some give two forms of the future tense: one for *simple futurity* and another for *determination*. As a matter of fact, however, the use of the auxiliaries *shall* and *will* with the infinitive is but one of several important methods of expressing the future and certainly does not deserve the title "the future tense." Some other combinations having a claim to be included in an English future tense are:

    (*a*) The verb *to be* + prepositional infinitive (He *is to go* with the committee.)

    (*b*) The verb *to be about* + prepositional infinitive (The man is *about to dive* from the bridge.)

    (*c*) The verb *to be* + *going* + prepositional infinitive (They *are going to go* by automobile.)

[13] Leonard, "Shall and Will," p. 497.

Then too, the *present form* of the verb frequently refers to future time both in subordinate clauses and in
independent sentences, when some other word than
the verb, or the context in general, indicates the time
idea (If it rains, I cannot go.) (He returns from his
trip tomorrow.)

On the other hand, the use of *shall* and *will* to express
determination (sometimes called "the emphatic future"
or "the colored future" or "the modal future") is no
more entitled to be included in the name "future tense"
than many other combinations of verbs, which, because
of their meaning, look to the future for fulfilment:

I desire to go	I mean to go
I want to go	I have to go
I need to go	I may go
I intend to go	I must go
I expect to go	I can go
I ought to go	I might go
I've got to go	I should go

The suggestion, then, which I should offer as the
means of accounting for the facts which we find concerning the expression of the future is this. The grounds
upon which the future is usually predicted are desire,
hope, intention, resolve, determination, compulsion, necessity, or possibility. Any locutions which express any
of these ideas related to the future may be taken up
and developed as future-tense signs. The course of
development is in the direction of their losing their
full word meanings and thus also losing their limitation
to the particular meanings suggested by their origin.
They tend to become future-tense signs but with color-
ings which range from an almost pure future sense to
distinctly modal ideas.[14]

3. I shall here give a survey of the principal ways in
which languages have come to possess expressions for
future time.

[14] Fries, "The Expression of the Future," p. 87.

(a) The present tense is used in the future sense.

(b) *Volition.* Both E. *will* and Dan. *vil* to a certain degree retain traces of the original meaning of real volition, and therefore E. *will go* cannot be given as a pure "future tense," though it approaches that function, as seen especially when it is applied to natural phenomena, as *it will certainly rain tonight.* There is also an increasing tendency to use *(wi)ll* in the first person instead of *shall,* as in *I'm afraid I'll die soon* (especially in Sc. and Mr.) which makes *will* even more the common auxiliary of the future.

(c) *Thought, intention.* O.N. *mun.* This cannot easily be kept apart from volition.

(d) *Obligation.* This is the original meaning of O. E. *sceal,* now *shall.* In English the meaning of obligation is restricted to the first person in assertions and to the second person in questions, although in some classes of subordinate clauses it is used in all three persons.

(e) *Motion.* Verbs meaning *go* and *come* are frequently used to indicate futurity. E. *I am going to write.*

(f) *Possibility.* E. *May* frequently denotes a somewhat vague futurity: *this may end in disaster.*[15]

4. John Fell, in his *Essays Towards an English Grammar,* 1784, apparently came closer than anybody in either the eighteenth or nineteenth centuries to describing the true status of *shall* and *will*: "*Will* as an auxiliary term, is a mere sign of futurity, set before the infinitive mode .... *shall,* even as an auxiliary sign always denotes something more than mere futurity, and constantly implies either obligation, possibility, contingency, or something conditional, and very often several of these together."[16]

---

[15] Jespersen, *Philosophy of Grammar,* pp. 160-161.
[16] Leonard, *Doctrine of Correctness in English Usage, 1700-1800,* pp. 73-74.

Shall and will in questions. Associated with the rules for *shall* and *will* in declarative sentences of future time there are parallel rules for the use of these words in questions. In his study of the use of *shall* and *will* in dramatic literature, Professor Fries finds the actual usage of these auxiliaries not entirely consistent with the traditional rules. He says of *shall* and *will* in questions: [17]

From these figures two conclusions seem evident:

1. The usual statement that *will* is *impossible* in questions of the first person is inaccurate, although it is true that *will* is seldom used in this situation. About three per cent of the instances in the first person appear with *will....*

2. The common statement regarding second person questions, for example that in the *New English Dictionary*, that in the second person "in categorical questions" *shall is* "normal" is, according to these figures, plainly inadequate. Of the 512 questions in the second person but 7 or 1.3 per cent use *shall;* all the rest employ *will.* Certainly *Shall you?* with its 7 cases out of 512 second person questions is no more *"normal"* than *Will I?* having 12 instances out of a total of 407 first person questions....

    One ought also to add here that there are a number of examples of *Will you?* in which the context seems to exclude from the word *will* the idea of "wish" or "resolve."

With this convincing evidence from Professor Fries' study it seems reasonable to expect the school-book rules for *shall* and *will* in questions to be greatly modified, perhaps to read, "In asking a question, *shall* is more generally used in the first person, although *will* is possible; in the second and third persons *will* is predominant."

[17] Fries, "The Periphrastic Future with *Shall* and *Will* in Modern English," pp. 1001-1003.

More evidence as to the preponderance of *will* or *shall* in everyday usage is furnished by a recent bulletin of the Bell Telephone System entitled, "The Words and Sounds of Telephone Conversations." In 79,390 spoken words, taken from conversations between two men, two women, or man and woman, a total of 1,900 conversations, the word *will* as an auxiliary was used 1,305 times in 402 conversations, while the word *shall* as an auxiliary was used but 6 times in 6 conversations.[18] That *shall* is exceedingly rare in common conversation seems established. That its use in literature, at least in dramatic literature, is not as common as is ordinarily supposed has been shown by Professor Fries. Upon what grounds, then, does a textbook author write, "Don't allow *will* to crowd *shall* out of your vocabulary"?[19]

Should and would. The textbooks agree with scarcely a dissenting voice that the rules applying to *shall* and *will* apply equally to *should* and *would*. The rules imply therefore that in simple declarative statements *should* is invariably used with the first person, and *would* with the second and third persons. In questions also, *should* is required in the first person, and either *should* or *would* in the second and third persons, depending upon the form expected in reply.

In addition to the auxiliary uses of *should* there are special modal uses not applicable to *shall*. These are (1) "In a conditional clause, the auxiliary is *should* for all persons except to indicate definite volition on the part of the subject of the clause." (2) "*Should* is frequently used like *ought* to express moral obligation."[20]

---

[18] French, Carter, and Koenig, pp. 14-15.
[19] John C. French, p. 346.
[20] Thomas, Manchester, and Scott, p. 550.

From this variety of uses, if the rules truly record the facts of usage, one expects to find the word *should* quite the equal of *would* with reference to frequency. Such, however, is not the case. The Bell Telephone System study reveals the facts that in a total of 1,900 conversations the word *would* occurs 379 times in 207 conversations (plus *wouldn't* 97 times in 79 conversations) while *should* was found but 50 times in 43 conversations.[21] It is only fair to assume from such figures that in ordinary colloquial usage *would* has assumed many of the functions of *should,* although not to the extent that *will* has replaced *shall.*

The use of *shall* and *will* as future auxiliaries, and to a lesser extent the use of *should* and *would,* have long engaged the attention of textbook writers. Much space has been devoted to a discussion of their "correct" use and many pages of exercises follow the discussions. In view of the evidence now available concerning these forms both from the standpoint of their history and their contemporary usage it seems advisable for textbooks in the elementary and junior high-school levels to follow the example of Kirby and Carpenter[22] and omit any discussion of "correct" usage for *shall, will, should* or *would.* Textbooks designed for the senior high school and college should either omit all reference to "correctness" or else give the whole story: traditions, rules, facts of past usage, and facts of present usage. Only by so doing can they pretend to any approximation to current usage.

Subjunctive mood. The disappearance of the distinctive forms of the subjunctive from modern English writing and speech is by no means a recent discovery. Priestly

[21] French, Carter, and Koenig, pp. 14-15.
[22] Kirby and Carpenter, Book VIII, p. 312.

writes in 1769, "Grammatical as this conjunctive (sub-junctive) form of verbs is said to be, by all who write upon the subject, it must, we think, be acknowledged, that it sometimes gives the appearance of stiffness, and harshness to a sentence." [23] Webster in 1798 says, " . . . by the construction in our language, no subjunctive mode is necessary—in most cases it is improper—and what is the strongest of all arguments, *it is not used in the spoken language,* which is the only true foundation of grammar." [24]

Of our own time, Professor Krapp writes in 1909.[25]

The most important contemporary change is that which is affecting the subjunctive mood. Practically, the only construction in Modern English in which the subjunctive is in living, natural use, is in the condition contrary to fact. . . . It seems likely, therefore, with the continuance of the present tendencies, that the subjunctive as a distinctive inflectional form will disappear, except, perhaps, in the one construction noted. Even here, however, the indicative form is used in a surprisingly large number of instances in good modern authors.

In similar vein is the statement of a modern educator: "The colloquial use of *if he was* is not at all uncommon among even the masters of language, and its use in the literature of great writers is so frequently seen that no one is justified in calling its use 'bad grammar.'" [26]

Many teachers, particularly instructors in college composition, insist that the subjunctive form in the conditional sentence contrary to fact is the only permissible one. Their contention is vigorously worded in an article appearing in the *Anglo-Saxon.* This writer says: [27]

[23] Leonard, *Doctrine of Correctness in English Usage, 1700-1800,* p. 203.

[24] *Ibid.,* p. 205.

[25] Krapp, *Modern English,* pp. 289-290.

[26] Cross, p. 328.

[27] Setzler, p. 4.

It may not be out of place to call attention . . . to the unwise practice of certain well-educated writers and speakers who make a habit of using the indicative instead of the subjunctive in the "if" clause of a conditional sentence contrary to fact ("unreal condition"); in saying, "If he was here, we would now begin the lesson" instead of, "If he were here, we would now begin the lesson." Some of these writers even go so far as to assert that the former sentence is equally correct and just as good English as the latter. But such a claim is without adequate basis. The use of "was" in the first sentence can make claim justly to only that inferior type of "correctness" which an illogical and inexact expression sometimes obtains through the frequency of its use by careless or uninformed writers and speakers.

This is the extreme position, which the writer sums up by saying, "The subjunctive mood, so far from being on the verge of disappearance, functions today with as much force and vitality as it ever did in any previous period of English history." [28]

This latter statement is probably true as far as the use of the subjunctive in America is concerned, but not in the sense that the writer intended. Never very firmly established (Webster said: "It is not used in the spoken language") despite the efforts of a century of school-masters, the distinctive subjunctive forms are today a literary grace by no means universally employed. The "unwise" writers who incur Setzler's ire include nearly all the masters of English literature, observant grammarians from the eighteenth century, and such contemporary linguists as Otto Jespersen, H. C. Wyld, George Curme, and G. P. Krapp. His "careless or uninformed" speakers include Franklin K. Lane, Henry Cabot Lodge, Theodore Roosevelt, and Calvin Coolidge, to mention only a few whose actual usage has been studied.[29]

[28] *Loc. cit.*
[29] Bevier, p. 207.

On the whole contemporary textbooks are inclined toward a liberal view of the subjunctive uses. What they fail to make clear is the fact that except for the use of *were* in conditions contrary to fact, all other uses of the subjunctive are extremely literary in tone and sometimes almost archaic.

The most common subjunctive forms are found in the use of *were* for *was* in such expressions as *if I were, if you were, if he were,* etc. and in the use of a *God forbid! Long live the king!* [30]

The last two uses from the statement above—"God forbid!" "Long live the king!"—are not truly subjunctive forms in modern English, but are really survivals of an ancient pattern now entirely lost from the language. Professor Jespersen points out the absurdity of saying, "Soon come the train," to express a wish. " . . . the sentence 'Long live the king' must therefore be analyzed as consisting of a formular 'Long live' which is living though the type is dead + a subject which is variable." [31]

Concerning the subjunctive mood in general, Jespersen says:

As a matter of fact, the history of English and Danish shows how the once flourishing subjunctive has withered more and more, until it now can be compared with those rudimentary organs whose use is problematic or very subordinate indeed. [32]

. . . in English in more than 90 per cent of the cases . . . the old preterit subjunctive is identical with the indicative, except in the singular of the one verb *be*, where *was* and *were* are still distinct. It is easy to understand, therefore, that the instinctive feeling for the difference between these two forms cannot be vivid enough to prevent the use of *was* where *were*

[30] Pearson and Kirchwey, pp. 493-494.
[31] Jespersen, *Philosophy of Grammar*, p. 20.
[32] *Ibid.*, p. 49.

would have been required some centuries ago. Since about 1700 *was* has been increasingly frequent in these positions. ... In literary language there has recently been a reaction in favor of *were*, which is preferred by most teachers; but in colloquial speech *were* is comparatively rare, except in the phrase "If I were you," and it is worth remarking that *was* is decidedly more emphatic than *were*, and thus may be said to mark the impossibility better than the old subjunctive form.[33]

An American observer notes, "Five of the greatest grammarians and about fifty authors from Baxter to the present show that *was* in the unreal condition and in the clause of 'wishing' is making inroads upon the territory of *were*. Whether we like it or not, such are the facts." [34]

It seems in accord with the facts to conclude that the subjunctive forms of verbs other than the verb *to be* constitute extremely formal literary usage verging on the archaic. With regard to the verb *to be* it may be concluded that the present tense "if he be" is a highly literary form, commonly supplanted by "if he is." In the past tense the form "if he were" is far more common in writing and cultivated speech although "if he was" is to all intents an equivalent form which may be considered standard English. The use of the subjunctive today becomes, therefore, more largely a question of taste than of "correctness."

THE ADVERB

The only question of grammatical form arising in connection with the modern English adverb is that of the adverbs formed without -*ly* as *hard, loud, soft, fast, slow,* sometimes called the "flat" adverbs. That some of these words are properly adverbs is not denied by any of the textbooks, but they disagree materially as to which ones

[33] *Ibid.*, pp. 266-267.
[34] J. Lesslie Hall, pp. 312-313.

of the list may be so accepted. One attempts an explanation of the reason for such adverbs, as follows: "A few (adverbs) formed by dropping an Old English inflectional -*e* have no ending: soon, fast." [35]

The determination of whether or not *loud, soft, fast, slow* are adverbs in a particular sentence is a question of syntax, but when one or more are categorically denied adverbial use the problem belongs properly to grammar. The words *loud* and *slow* are specifically excepted from the lists of adverbs by three authors, and form, therefore, the examples for this discussion.

The following example of incorrect grammar is cited by one author. "The bell, ringing *loud,* was heard by all." [36] One cannot fail to note with interest that two of the writers cited just above include *loud* in their lists of adverbs, one in fact using it as the only example. The word *slow,* on the other hand, receives only silent objection, no author defending it, although it is the most commonly used of these adverbs. The advent of the automobile, necessitating the caution "drive *slow,*" has placed this usage before the eyes of everyone. It is discouraging to note that a recent textbook devotes the most space to destroying *slow* as an adverb, giving half a page to a graphic representation of this supposed fault. It is this sort of wholesale denial of current usage, though the usage is backed up by the history of the word and the authority of the *New English Dictionary,* that destroys the value of textbooks as guides to contemporary speech.

Another author resorts to a doubtful argument to distinguish between the adjective and adverb. In the sentence, "He rolled the cigarette *tight,*" the word *tight* is an adjective because "The state of the cigarette when

[35] John C. French, p. 288.
[36] McFadden and Ferguson, p. 308.

rolled was that of tightness." [37] But in the command "Hold on tight!" one suspects that if the holder were "tight," he might fail to obey the command. This illustration is cited not so much to defend the use of *tight* as an adverb as to point out the speciousness of the argument.

Returning now to the main question, what rule, if any, governs the choice of the alternative adverb forms *loud, loudly, soft, softly, slow, slowly,* and the rest? The problem is by no means a recent one, as is shown by the fact that Dr. Samuel Johnson "lists words like *slow* as adjectives only,[38] in direct defiance of the contrary usage of Milton and others. The real solution is suggested by Leonard in his canons for the determination of usage. "Euophony seems rarely to have been appealed to for resolution of problems like the use of *slow* or *slowly*, *feel bad* or *badly*, and the like, which probably are actually settled to fit sentence cadence." [39] For textbook purposes the matter might be stated thus: some adverbs have two forms, one identical with the adjective of similar meaning, as *loud, soft, quick, slow,* and the other formed with *-ly*, as *loudly, softly, quickly, slowly*. Either form is grammatically correct, but the sound of the adverb in the sentence determines to some extent which form to select. Hence in imperative sentences, "Come quick," "Drive slow," and "Speak soft," the shorter form is quite generally used; in declarative sentences, "We walked slowly," "They spoke softly," the longer form is more frequently used. In any type of sentence the sound of the adverb in the sentence is the determining factor.

This section cannot better conclude than with a line

[37] Raymond, p. 197.
[38] Leonard, *Doctrine of Correctness in English Usage, 1700-1800*, p. 70.
[39] *Ibid.*, p. 155.

from a poem of Arthur Hugh Clough, who says, "In front the sun climbs slow, how slowly." [40] What could more clearly exhibit the parallel forms of the adverb, side by side in a parallel construction, the position of both forms being determined solely by euphony!

THE NOUN

The grammar of the English noun has become so simple through the inflectional losses of the ages that little remains to cause difficulty or difference. The plural forms of a few foreign or uncommon words, the question of popular, or "ungrammatical" gender, and the use of some possessive forms constitute the items for consideration in this section.

Number. How are the plural forms of foreign nouns made? Must they follow the grammar of their native languages or may they be naturalized into English? The answers to these questions once provided the grammar books with several pages of material. The attitude of the past quarter-century as revealed by textbooks shows a decidedly liberal attitude toward the naturalization of commonly used foreign words.

In this instance the statements of the text writers concur with the facts of current usage. The plural form of a foreign word is determined solely by its *use* in English. Hence *memorandums, curriculums, genuses,* and *indexes* may exist peaceably side by side with *memoranda, curricula, genera, indices.* If other foreign words become as much at home in our language as these, they too may have English plurals. But if the foreign plural of a popular foreign word also becomes popular, as in the

[40] Arthur H. Clough, *Poems* (London, 1869), Vol. II, p. 497.

case of *alumnus, alumni, datum, data,* the foreign plural is established, logic and consistency notwithstanding.

The word *data* is of peculiar interest because it is apparently becoming popularized with a new use and meaning. Originally a foreign plural of a foreign noun, it is rapidly changing into a collective noun in the singular number, so that the expression "This data is" instead of "These data are" is by no means uncommon. The word thus used means "information," "collection of facts," or "results of investigation." If such a word is needed, and it seems to be so needed, no one can object to a singular *data* who regularly uses the singular "news" from a former plural *news,* or a singular *links* (a golf *links*) from a former plural *links.*

Are the words *mathematics, physics, politics, athletics* singular or plural? Those textbook writers who treat of the matter at all favor the singular.

(*a*) Some nouns plural in form are now generally used as singulars; as—*economics, physics, mathematics, politics.*[41]

(*b*) Some nouns have no plural form. This is true of *measles, news, mathematics.* Consult the dictionary for *athletics,* and *politics.*[42]

A comparison of the rule for the number of the word *mathematics* in references (*a*) and (*b*) above reveals the paradox that *mathematics* is a plural used as a singular, and it is also a singular that has no plural. It is small wonder that school children are perplexed by matters in which the authorities placed before them differ so widely.

Webster's *Collegiate Dictionary,* edition of 1929, says of these words: "When denoting a scientific treatise, or

[41] Hyde, p. 37.
[42] Kimball, Book II, p. 53.

its subject matter, forms in -ics are construed in the singular; as, mathematics, physics; but those denoting matters of practice, as gymnastics, tactics, are oftener construed as plurals."

The foregoing definition fails to afford much help in the case of *politics* which may be considered either a scientific treatise and its subject matter or a matter of practice. As a matter of practice the word is regularly used in the plural, though there is equal authority for its use in the singular. J. Lesslie Hall quotes Emerson: "The politics *are* base," and Chesteron: "Politics in *its* historic aspect would seem to have had a great fascination for him...." Hall sums up the discussion of the words in -*ics* as follows: [43]

The tendency in words in -*ics* is to take the singular regimen; such has been the case with *mathematics, ethics, physics, optics;* but *athletics* and *politics* seem to prefer the plural. An impartial study of *politics* from Queen Anne's day to the present shows that it is prevailing plural, plural in more than three-fourths of the passages in which it is found. Further reading, however, might change the figures to some extent.

Gender. The following description of English gender is common to the texts treating of the subject. "The distinction between words to denote sex is called *gender*. A noun that denotes a male is of the *masculine* gender; a noun that denotes a female is of the *feminine* gender; a noun that may denote either a male or a female is of the *common* gender; a noun that denotes a thing neither male nor female is of the *neuter* gender." [44]

These rules are true enough as far as they go, but they fail to recognize a popular or "ungrammatical" use of gender which is so common as to be part of the idiom of

[43] J. Lesslie Hall, pp. 199-202.
[44] Hyde, Book II, p. 42

almost every speaker of English. This phenomenon is the regular use of *she* or *her* to refer to inanimate objects. A few examples serve to recall how common the usage is.

1. Automobile owner working on his car:
   "I've got *her* going!"

2. "Here *she* comes!" speaking of a train or ship.

3. "*She's* a grand old country," speaking of a nation or political division.

Svartengren has made a study of this phenomenon in English, saying, "The use of the feminine for inanimate objects is native—masculine in character—and quite widespread. The *she* seems to be regularly used with three classes of nouns:

I. Concrete things made or worked upon by man

II. Actions, abstract ideas

III. Nature, and natural objects not worked upon by man [45]

Professor Curme also notes that "We are inclined to make *church, university, state,* and especially *ship* feminine. With a good deal of persistency we say of a ship: 'She behaves well, *she* minds her rudder, *she* swims like a duck. . . . '" [46] While this use of the feminine gender is not a point to be labored, it scarcely seems right to neglect it utterly in all textbooks describing the grammar of English. Somewhere in the sections on gender there should be mention of so widespread and common a use of the feminine forms.

The possessive case. "Names of inanimate objects should rarely be put in the possessive case, for it is confusing to think of inanimate objects as possessing—having

[45] Svartengren, p. 83.
[46] Curme, *Syntax*, p. 556.

ownership in—anything. Instead of the possessive forms, make use of a phrase, generally with *of*." [47]

The rule for the use of the noun in the possessive case, limiting its function to living things in prose, and personified objects in verse, is quite commonly found in the school grammars. It is quite clearly stated in the grammar of Kittredge and Farley where it appears thus, "In older English, and in poetry, the possessive case of nouns is freely used, but in modern prose it is rare unless the possessor is a living being." [48]

It goes without saying that the genitive in *s* is the older form in English. In the *Beowulf* we find "Hares hyrste" (Hair's ornaments); "non daeges" (day's noon); "heofenes haðor" (heaven's receptacle); and in the *Voyages of Othere and Wulfstan* the phrase, "ðaes landes sceawunge" (for the land's spying out); and "aelces geðeodes man" (each tribe's man). From Chaucer come also "my hertes lady," "lyves light," "worldes richesse" and many others.

In more recent times it is true that the *of* construction has largely replaced the older -*s* genitive, but not to the point of utter exclusion. There seems to be no justification either in the history of the form or in current usage for the rule that "the possessive case is properly used only with names of living beings," or for the series of exercises in grammar books in which such useful forms as "the house's roof," "the clock's hands," "the room's length" are offered for correction. As a matter of fact, certain established patterns such as "a hair's breadth," "an arm's length," "a stone's throw" cannot be transposed to the *of* construction without doing violence to the meaning, since the phrases "the breadth of a hair," "the length

[47] Raymond, p. 192.
[48] Kittredge and Farley, p. 45.

of an arm," and "the throw of a stone" will not serve in the place of the possessive constructions.

Hall presents a table showing 700 passages containing the possessive use with things without life, from 87 authorities from John Mandeville to H. W. Mabie. Commenting on this table, he says, "It would be impossible to exhaust this subject; the number of passages could be increased indefinitely. It is almost impossible to read any good book by a reputable writer without seeing this interdicted locution at frequent intervals; the rule is not based upon the literature." [49]

With such overwhelming evidence from the literature of the past, together with the corroborative examples in the current periodicals of the better sort, it seems advisable to substitute a more modern statement concerning the possessive case with inanimate objects than that which now obtains in the grammars. It might be worded: Possession is indicated in two ways in English: (1) by the use of the possessive case, and (2) by the use of the *of* phrase. The possessive case is more generally used with proper nouns and the names of living or personified objects, though there are many examples in standard literature of the possessive case used with inanimate objects. The *of* phrase, however, is more commonly used with inanimate objects to show possession. In cases of doubt select the form most consistent with euphony.

THE PRONOUN

I—me. There was a time in the history of the English language when an honest grammarian would have been

[49] J. Lesslie Hall, pp. 204-206. Two examples from current reading come to mind. Warwick Deeping in *Sorrel and Son* says, "They closed it [the door] carefully, as though the *room's* emptiness...." From a magazine comes, "A ... conference of *three pints of Bourbon and one-half box of cigar's duration.*"

compelled to report, concerning pronoun usage, a social distinction becoming more and more felt in the use of the second person singular pronouns. The hypothetical grammarian would have written, "thou dost well"—common or uncultivated usage; "you do well"—cultivated, polite usage. Since that time the more formal usage has prevailed until the original second person singular has been relegated to the language of poetry, religion, and secret societies. As a result "you do well," addressed to one person, is obsolete grammar but good usage; "thou dost well" is good grammar but obsolete usage.

To what extent, then, can the appeal to logical form be urged against the increasingly common usage "It is me"? Custom, which made *you* a singular pronoun in correct usage, is just as surely establishing the combination "it is me," grammar and logic notwithstanding. The textbooks, however, recognize neither the process nor the result.

The failure of the school texts to make some allowance for common usage is the more surprising in view of the long history of "it is me" and the quantities of print that it has evoked in attack and defense. Priestly writing in 1762, says: [50]

All our grammarians say that the nominative case of pronouns ought to follow the verb substantive (*is*, and the like) as well as precede it; yet many familiar forms of speech, and the example of some of our best writers, would lead us to make a contrary rule; or, at least, would leave us at liberty to adopt which we like best: *Are these the houses? Yes, they are* them. *Who is There? It is* me. *It is* him. *It is not* me *you are in love with* (Addison). *It cannot be* me (Swift). *To that which once was* thee (Prior). *There is but one man that she can have, and that is* me (*Clarissa*).

[50] Quoted in Leonard, *Doctrine of Correctness in English Usage, 1700-1800,* p. 186.

Professor Krapp, in his *Guide* conveys a tone of doubt and uncertainty regarding the position of "it is me." After listing some examples he says: [51]

Nevertheless the preponderance of theoretical opinion is not on the side either of *me*, or of *her*, *him*, etc., as nominatives. . . . By the historical rules of grammar such constructions are incorrect. But this test in itself is not decisive, for many uses now in good standing are historically incorrect. The question is whether these particular uses have established themselves as correct beyond debate. The answer to this question must obviously be in the negative. . . .

The Leonard-Moffett study, however, reveals a far more widespread acceptance of "it is me" than Professor Krapp's article would indicate. The linguists rated at 2.1 on a scale of 4 points, in which point 2 represents "cultivated informal English." It must be added, though, that other groups of judges were more conservative, as the following table shows:

On a scale of 4 points in which 1 represents "literary or formal English" and 4 "uncultivated English," the average rating of "it is me" for

23 Authors	was	3.2
24 Editors	was	3.2
24 Business men	was	3.6
68 Members of the M.L.A.	was	2.4
50 Members of the English Council	was	2.9
12 Teachers of Speech	was	2.5

Here, as in many other instances, the students of language were more liberal in accepting the usage than were other educated groups.[52]

Commenting upon the findings of this study, an editorial in the London *Evening Standard* says: [53]

[51] Krapp, *Comprehensive Guide to Good English*, p. 382.
[52] Leonard and Moffett, p. 353.
[53] London *Evening Standard*, October 8, 1927.

There are two ways of defending [it is me]. One is to point out that "me" here is not the accusative "me," but the equivalent, and probably a survival, of the French "moi." Just as the French do not say "C'est je" or, in answer to a question, simply "Je!" so we—unless we are ultra-particular—do not say "it's I" or simply "I!". We say "it's me," or "Me!" and we do it for the same reasons and the same justification.

The other way of defending it is to remark that language preceded grammarians, and still takes precedence of them. The business of the grammarian is to observe, perhaps to explain, accomplish facts. But the facts themselves are outside his power. . . . Either, or both, of these defences may be right. The history of linguistics shows that languages will grow in spite of all attempts to restrain them. What seems to be the solecism of today is the accepted idiom of tomorrow.

Havelock Ellis joins forces with the defenders of "it is me." [54]

But there are other points at which some, even good critics (that lets you out!) may be tempted to accept the commendation of the literary grammarians. It is sufficient to mention one: the nominative use of the pronoun "me." Yet surely, anyone who considers social practice as well as psychological necessity should not fail to see that we must recognize a double use of "me" in English. The French, who in such matters seem to have possessed a finer social and psychological tact, have realized that "je" cannot be the sole nominative of the first person and have supplemented it by "moi" ("mi" from "mihi"). The Frenchman, when asked who is there, does not reply "Je!" but the would-be purist in English is supposed to be reduced to replying "I!" Royal Cleopatra asks the Messenger: "Is she as tall as me?" The would-be purist no doubt transmutes this as he reads into "Is she as tall as I?" We need not envy him.

Mr. Ellis strikes at the heart of the controversy in his use of the terms "social practice" and "psychological necessity." These are the bases of correct usage, though perhaps in reverse order. "Psychological necessity" estab-

[54] Ellis, p. 140.

lishes a "social practice" in language, which will triumph over logic and the grammar of former days despite the howls of purists and the rods of schoolmasters. Many such "psychological necessities" are now "correct" usage; many more will be as their need is felt.

The honest textbook writer of the future must face the facts. He must bow to social custom. In his discussion of the first person singular pronoun after the verb *to be* he must say: In formal literary, and solemn style the pronoun *I* is used; in cultivated colloquial usage custom has also established the pronoun *me*. The tone and purpose of the speech or writing must in all cases determine the choice of the pronoun.

It is him, her. Although extremely common in the less cultivated levels of current English, and occurring sporadically in standard literature, (as in "somebody leaner and darker than him" in Lord Dunsany's *The Blessing of Pan*) the pronouns *him* and *her* in nominative constructions have far less standing and support than does *me* in similar constructions. This fact is an interesting illustration of the validating force of custom. Logically, if "it is me" is accepted, "it is him" or "her" must be similarly accepted, as they are parallel constructions. But custom, not logic, rules, discriminating clearly between the acceptable "it is me" and the excluded "it is her, him." It is possible, too, that the customary telephone reply, "This is he (she) speaking," has had an influence in preserving the nominative forms.

The *New English Dictionary* acknowledges this usage historically as follows:

> *him.* For the nominative especially after *than, as* and in predicate after *be.* Common in colloquial language from the end of the 16th century. Dia-

lectically the use of *him* for *he* extends to all constructions in which French uses *lui* for *il*. It has
been used thus by Chaucer, Shakespeare, Van
Brugh, Johnson, Tucker, and Burke, to name only
a few.

The judges of the Leonard-Moffett study found the
usage "I am older than *him*" far less acceptable than "it
is *me*." The latter usage was ranked 25th in a list of 102
items arranged in order of acceptability, while "I am
older than *him*" was ranked 87th.

Professor Krapp says of the nominative uses of *her,
him, them*: "Though widely current, these uses do not
have the sanction of authority, and are usually designated
as incorrect by grammarians and other critics of speech.
. . . It is possible that in time general use will make these
constructions so customary that they will be accepted as
correct, but that time has not yet arrived." [55]

The foregoing statement summarizes the uses of *her,
him, them* adequately. These forms are common, but not
in written English nor cultivated speech. The chief fact
to stress is that they do not have the standing of "it is
me," and that the establishment of the latter in current
acceptable English does not constitute support for them
in any way. Each usage must be judged on its own
merits.

Who and whom. Such sentences as "*Who* did they
punish?" "*Who* did you give it to?" "*Who* are you going
to invite?" are quite generally condemned in current textbooks as examples of bad grammar and incorrect usage.
Such wholesale condemnation is by no means representative of current usage, as any careful observer of cultivated speech and informal writing can readily testify. In

[55] Krapp, *Comprehensive Guide to Good English*, p. 298.

the initial position in questions, *who* is far more prevalent than *whom* even though it may be grammatically the object of a following verb or preposition. On the contrary, when the pronoun immediately follows the verb or preposition cultivated usage requires the objective form as in "For whom was it sent?" "You saw whom?". The use of the nominative in the initial position seems to be the result of certain inherent language habits, one of which is the feeling for a nominative form of the beginning of a sentence and another the reluctance to make a grammatical decision before the context requires it.[56] One observer reports: " . . . all cultivated persons unless they make a heroic and conscious effort invariably say '*Who* is it for?' and '*Who* did you see?' . . . On the contrary no cultivated person says 'a man *who* I saw'; almost invariably one says 'a man I saw,' or less often, 'a man that I saw.' " [57] In the eighteenth century the use of *who* for *whom* was condemned by Lowth, Buchanan, Hornsey, and Bingham, but was defended by Webster and Priestly.[58] The American grammarian, Webster, strangely enough calls on analogy with Latin grammar for his defense, although he usually avoided classical analogy in his treatment of usage. He says: [59]

. . . "*whom* did you speak *to?*" was never used in speaking, as I can find, and if so, is hardly English at all. There is no doubt, in my mind, that the English *who* and the Latin *qui*

[56] This latter habit is interestingly revealed in *The Blessing of Pan*, by Lord Dunsany. The speaker makes an inquiry: " 'Who?' said the Vicar. 'Whom do you mean?' " The repetition of the interrogative pronoun gives time for a grammatical decision—to use the objective form. The first is spontaneous and is grammatically undecided, or nominative.

[57] Leonard, "Educational Quackery," p. 806.

[58] Quoted in Leonard, *Doctrine of Correctness in English Usage, 1700-1800*, p. 263.

[59] *Ibid.*, pp. 51-52.

are the same word with mere variations of dialect. *Who* in the Gothic and Teutonic, has always answered to the nominative *qui;* and dative *cui* which was pronounced like *qui,* and the ablative *quo.*

. . . So that *Who* did he speak *to?* *Who* did you go *with?* were probably as good English, in ancient times, as *Cui dixit? Cum quo ivisti?* in Latin. Nay it is more than probable that *who* was once wholly used in asking questions, even in the objective case; *Who* did he marry? until some Latin student began to suspect it bad English, because it was not agreeable to the Latin rules. At any rate, *Whom* do you speak *to?* is a corruption and all the grammars that can be found will not extend the use of the phrase beyond the walls of a college.

The modern linguist is scarcely prepared to agree with Webster that the dative use of *whom* is a corruption, nor to defend wholeheartedly this etymology, sound though it is in part, but his final statement that a usage based upon logic or analogy with Latin grammar "will not extend the use of a phrase beyond the walls of a college" commands respect as the observation of a genuine student of language with an objective viewpoint remarkable in his day. As a matter of fact, *who* has been used as an objective form throughout the history of English. The *New English Dictionary* says, "Common in colloquial use as the object of a verb, or of a preposition following at the end of a clause," and lists examples from Cranmer to Hardy.

The anxiety of textbook writers to correct the faulty *who* leads occasionally to absurdities. Of such a character is the following, "In questions, *whom* comes at the beginning of the sentence, where we ordinarily find the subject." [60] There is no limiting or modifying statement, leading the student naturally to the assumption that every question employing the interrogative pronoun must begin

[60] Kirby and Carpenter, Book VIII, p. 32.

with *whom*. He therefore says, or writes, in good faith "*Whom* are you?" and "*Whom* did you think I was?"

The discussion thus far has dealt with *who* and *whom* as interrogative pronouns. As relative pronouns they give rise to several interesting constructions. The use of *who* as a relative pronoun in an objective construction is far less common in cultivated speech and writing, chiefly because, as Professor Leonard points out (see footnote 57) in freer use the pronoun tends to be omitted entirely, as in "That is the man I saw," or the uninflected *that* is substituted, as in "Garrick was the actor that I referred to." Nevertheless, the use of *who* as an objective relative is by no means rare. A recent letter from the editorial rooms of the Rand McNally and Company, publishers, contains the sentence, "This copy editor, however, is no pedant but an up-to-date broad-minded college woman *who* we can usually trust to go ahead and prepare a manuscript without special supervision." Such a sentence in a letter from a mercantile firm would have small significance, but from an editor in the employ of a prominent publishing house (a person professionally "language-minded") it reveals the fact that even to a professional writer *who* in this sentence awoke no grammatical consciousness, but was natural and spontaneous.

The case of the relative pronoun in such sentences as "There is a man *who* I know will be faithful," is sometimes disputed. *Who* is ordinarily parsed as the subject of the verb *will be,* the clause *I know* being considered parenthetical. Some writers, perhaps influenced by the stress on the objective *whom* in the schoolroom, use *whom* in such a sentence, making it objective of the verb *know.* An example occurs in Richard Haliburton's *Royal Road to Romance,* p. 152: "men . . . *whom* I knew would excommunicate their erstwhile shipmates. . . . " While such usages do occur, they are by no means common enough to challenge seriously the customary nominative *who*.

Except in strictly formal writing the compounds *whoever* and *whosoever* are in current usage quite generally employed as nominative and objective forms. The reason lies in the grammatical uncertainty connected with the usual syntax of these forms, that of an object of a preceding verb or preposition, and subject to a succeeding verb. This sentence from Boswell's *Life of Johnson* illustrates the point very well, " . . . you shall meet whoever comes, for me." Is *whoever* in this sentence object of the verb *meet* or subject of the verb *comes*? Of course it is in a sense both, but Boswell undoubtedly felt the subject relation to be the stronger and wrote it so. The nominative gains further support when it is realized that the object of *meet* is really an objective *him*, which is omitted for convenience but may be readily reinstated, as in, "You shall meet *him*, whoever comes," or "I shall punish *him*, whoever speaks." When a preposition immediately precedes, the dilemma is stronger. "This is addressed to whoever is concerned." Here again the phrase "whoever is concerned" is felt to be the entire object of the preposition rather than *whoever* alone, and is consequently made nominative rather than objective. On the other hand, the objective form is sometimes employed in a similar construction, thus: " . . . admired by *whomsoever* shall happen upon these lines." (From *Anthology of Pure Poetry* by George Moore, p. 7). As a result of these doubtful constructions, the compound relative pronouns tend to be used nominatively even when the grammar is clear, as in "I will go with whoever I like," simply because in nearly all constructions even with a preposition *whoever* is used nominatively. The school-books are quite right in distinguishing the case forms for the compound relative pronouns for strictly literary usage, but to insist that these literary and formal distinctions be made in informal writing and speech as necessary "correctness" is to do violence to the readily observed facts of current usage. It has been shown, moreover, that even in literary usage the forms are not indisputable.

VII

Problems in English Syntax

It is the purpose of this chapter to demonstrate that the rules of the ordinary school textbooks with regard to syntactical problems are often at variance with the usage of standard literature or the customs of polite society. That these rules are frequently of long standing and carry the weight of some authority is not disputed; it is rather the contention of this chapter that they are "prescriptive" in the sense that they represent what their authors feel should be, in contradiction to what actually is in literary and current usage. As is the case in the preceding chapter on prescriptive grammar, no attempt is made to present a complete survey of English syntax, but instead to select from textbooks certain clear and concrete issues unequivocally presented by their authors which may be dealt with objectively. It follows, therefore, that the items dealt with in this chapter cannot be grouped very conveniently into categories except that different problems affecting a particular part of speech may be placed under one heading. While the general terms "concord," "word order," and so forth, would cover a number of the specific items, there would remain too many miscellaneous ungrouped items to make such a scheme of organization feasible. For that reason each general item has been listed separately without regard for the order usually observed in works on syntax.

SUBJECT-VERB AGREEMENT

Many textbooks declare flatly that "a verb must agree in number with its subject." As there are no explanatory statements attached to the rule, the student is forced to conclude that every verb in English must agree with the *form* of the subject in number, regardless of the meaning or intention. The examples offered to illustrate the rules all tend to reinforce this conclusion. But the users of English all through its history have never felt constrained to observe formal concord; they have made their verbs agree with the feeling or intention of the subject no matter what the form. "In the Anglo-Saxon period, we see plural subjects taking the singular verb . . . the writer has recorded four unmistakable cases in *Beowulf*. . . . In Chaucer's *Squire's Tale* we read 'The spyces and the wyn is come anon'. . . . Malory says, 'was chosen . . . the most men of worship.' These are typical of numerous passages in Malory, Latimer, Marlowe, Shakespeare, and many Elizabethan authors." [1]

Milton also used free syntax in subject-predicate agreement; so did Cowley, Swift, Defoe, Hume, Lamb, Thackeray, and indeed almost every writer of note to the middle of the nineteenth century. From that time on, however, the rules of the eighteenth century became rigid in the formalism of the nineteenth, with a resultant closer attention to formal agreement. But examples of freer usage as in Kipling's "The tumult and the shouting dies," if not common, still serve to remind us that formal agreement in the subject-verb relationship may be violated when the sense of the expression is stronger than the feeling for concord. From the literature it appears that concord was settled entirely by the meaning of the

[1] J. Lesslie Hall, *English Usage*, pp. 53-54.

passage prior to the eighteenth century, as is witnessed by Shakespeare's very free use; in the eighteenth century regimentation set in, only slightly affecting the writers of that century but greatly influencing the practice of the succeeding century, so that the earlier freedom very largely, though not entirely, disappeared. But many problems were left unsolved by the rules.

In this connection the comment of Jespersen is illuminating: [2]

Those languages which have kept the old rule of concord in secondary words are very often thereby involved in difficulties, and grammars have to give more or less intricate rules which are not always observed in ordinary life... even by the "best writers." A few English quotations (taken from M.E.G. II, Ch. VI) will show the nature of such difficulties with verbs:

> not one in ten of them *write* so badly
> ten *is* one and nine
> none *has* more keenly felt them
> neither of your friends *are* safe
> if the death of neither man nor gnat *are* designed
> one or two of his things *are* still worth your reading
> his meat *was* locusts and wild honey
> both death and I *am* found eternal

All these sentences are taken from well-known writers, the last, for instance from Milton.

It is with these points of possible difficulty that we now deal, assorting them into distinct categories for greater convenience and clarity. The classification is not exhaustive inasmuch as the items listed are only those subject to definite rules in the school texts.

1. *The verb with the compound subject.* Textbook rule: "Two or more singular subjects connected by *and*

[2] Jespersen, *Philosophy of Grammar*, p. 209.

require a plural verb."[3] While it is generally true in modern usage that a compound subject joined by *and* is followed by a plural verb, there are notable exceptions which cannot be ignored. For example, when a compound subject refers to one person, as in "My old friend and adviser *is* sick," the verb is always singular because the subject, though plural in form, is actually singular. Likewise when a series of subjects is arranged in climactic order the verb tends to agree with the last subject because of its emphasis, as in "Your families, your homes, your country *calls* you to serve!" When a compound subject follows the verb, the verb is very often in the singular, as in "There is wealth and glory for the man who will do this." This usage is more common after "there is," "there exists," and so forth, as Curme remarks: "Survivals still occasionally occur also in literary language after *there is, there exists*, etc., i.e., in certain set expressions where the mind is not on the alert";[4] although the explanation probably lies more in the accepted pattern of "there is" plus a plural subject than in any lack of alertness of mind. Since the "there is" combination is followed in the great majority of sentences by a singular subject it has become a standard way of introducing a subject, whether singular or plural, another example of the victory of usage over logical grammar. So well intrenched is this that the overmeticulous plural verb is uncomfortably conspicuous in the sentence, as in: "But what interests Sutter beyond all else *are* the stories brought him by travelers." (Henry L. Stewart, *Harpers Magazine,* January, 1926.) Needless to say, the verb *is* would pass without notice in this sentence.

Several years ago a most amusing and at the same time

---

[3] Pearson and Kirchwey, p. 153.
[4] Curme, *Syntax*, p. 55.

significant controversy arose out of a sentence used by the Burlington Railroad in an advertisement. The sentence ran, "For within this tremendous area *is* produced: two-thirds the oats, more than half the corn, more than half the barley, half the wheat, half the hogs, nearly half the cattle, nearly half the gold, wool and cotton." [5] The question of whether *is* or *are* was correct in this sentence aroused national interest. Upon appeal the *Literary Digest* and Professor Phelps of Yale voted for *are*; Professor R. K. Root of Princeton and Bliss Perry of Harvard voted for *is*. The press took up the discussion with editorials, news stories, and features. The question was of course not settled and never will be until either rule or usage becomes absolute.

In all the examples cited the number of the verb is clearly a matter of agreement with the *feeling* for number in the subject. Instead of the iron-clad rule, "Two or more singular subjects connected by *and* require a plural verb," the rule should be stated: Two or more subjects joined by *and* when felt to be plural are followed by a plural verb; when the subject, though plural in form, is felt to be a single entity, the singular verb may be used; when the compound subject follows the verb, the verb is frequently in the singular, especially in the patterns "there is," "there exists."

2. *Singular subjects formed with* or, nor. Textbook rule: "When two singular subjects are connected by *or* or *nor*, the subject is singular and the singular form of the verb should be used." [6] In such a sentence as "The president or the secretary is expected to do this work," the singular nature of the subject is preserved and the verb accordingly agrees. But in the sentence, "Frank or

[5] Burlington Railroad, p. 3.
[6] Pearson and Kirchwey, p. 153.

Jim *have* come on alternate weeks to my at-homes," the
subject is really plural in idea though singular in form.
Hence with *or* or *nor* connecting two subjects there is
greater freedom observed in the verb agreement, despite
the fact that strict logic demands the singular. This fact
is especially true in questions, in which the singular verb
though logically correct is so unusual as to be conspicuous. For example, "*Is* Frank or Jim here?" "*Has* father
or mother come in yet?" In these sentences the singular
verb is distressingly odd where the plural would pass
unnoticed. Curme points out also the tendency to use the
plural verb with negative statements having a compound
subject: "After *neither . . . nor* we still often find the
plural verb after singular subjects since there has long
been a tendency to give formal expression to the plural
idea which always lies in the negative form of statement." [7] He offers a number of examples, a few of which
follow. "Neither search nor labor *are* necessary," (Johnson); "Neither he nor his lady *were* at home." (George
Washington); "Neither painting nor fighting *feed* men."
(Ruskin) [8]

It is quite evident that the rule, "When two singular
subjects are joined by *or* or *nor,* the subject is singular
and the singular form of the verb should be used" needs
considerable revision. Any rule formulated for this case
must point out (1) that two singular subjects joined by
or or *nor* when felt to be singular and alternative are
followed by a singular verb; (2) that when they are felt
to be plural or grouped, are followed by a plural verb;
(3) that in questions the plural verb is almost always
used; and (4) that in negative statements the plural verb
is very common. All of these uses, unconsciously em-

[7] Curme, *Syntax,* p. 56.
[8] *Loc. cit.*

ployed by the rule-makers themselves, rarely enter the school-books.

3. *The singular subject with plural modification.* Textbook rule: "A verb agrees in number with its subject, regardless as to whether or not a noun or nouns intervene between the verb and its subject." [9] If this rule were changed to read, "A verb agrees with the intended number of its subject, even though the form differ," it would be much closer to the truth. When a singular noun (singular in form) is followed by a modifier, especially a partitive group (which) conveys the idea of plurality ... the verb is in the plural, even though the governing noun is singular...." [10] We frequently see such sentences as "A great heap of books *are* on my table"; "The entire list of candidates *were* interviewed"; "During 1931, $876,868.00 worth of books *were* distributed free." From this common free use of the plural idea expressed by a singular noun followed by a partitive modifier, we are not greatly surprised to find H. C. Wyld, the noted English linguist, saying in his *Historical Study of the Mother Tongue*, "Thus in time the aggregate of impressions *result* in a memory picture...."

4. *A singular subject augmented by phrases introduced by* with, together with, as well as, no less than, *etc.* Textbook rule: "Parenthetical expressions introduced by words such as *with, as well as, no less than,* and the like do not affect the number of the verb." [11] Ordinarily in such sentences the augmentation of the subject is so distinctly parenthetical as to be without influence on the number of the subject, so that a singular noun, though augmented, is followed by a singular verb. But occasion-

[9] Raymond, p. 199.
[10] Curme, *Syntax*, p. 51.
[11] Raymond, p. 199.

ally the augmentation is distinctly cumulative, as though the secondary idea were attached by *and,* in which case a plural verb is sometimes employed. Similarly, when the secondary idea stresses plural number, the plural verb often follows. So we find generally: "John, together with some friends, *was* here yesterday"; but, "The captain as well as most of his men *were* never seen again"; and "Old Sir John with half-a-dozen men *are* at the door." Further examples: "...the count, with my nephew and me, *were* introduced by his son...." (Smollett); "Comparative phonetics, as well as experimental phonetics, *are* covered." (G. W. Gray, *Quarterly Journal of Speech,* November, 1931, p. 593.) Here again as in the cases previously cited the verb agreement is dependent upon the concept of number in the subject rather than upon the form.

5. *Collective nouns.* Textbook rule: "A collective noun takes a singular or a plural verb, according as the collection is thought of as a whole or as composed of individuals. The committee *have* disagreed. The common council *was* called to order." [12] In this instance the textbook rules correctly report English usage, which in the case of the collective noun has always formed the verb in agreement with the implied number of the subject. So strongly is this agreement felt, that in colloquial speech and informal writing the noun actually changes number within a single sentence as it is variously considered in its group and individual aspects. Thus in a newspaper article we find, "Most of the throng *which* will attend, if the two student bodies are expected, *care* little who wins, and *is* attending for the spectacle *it hopes* to see." *Throng* is first considered as a group and is modified by *which;* it is next considered as a collection of individuals

[12] Brooks, p. 125.

who "care little who wins"; then it becomes again a group in the singular with singular verbs and a pronoun in agreement. While this sentence cannot be advanced as a model of English syntax, it is indeed an interesting example of the psychological aspects of grammatical concord. One is tempted to raise the question, Does not a sentence like this contain more subtle shades of meaning than one in which the collective noun is held singular or plural throughout for the sake of grammatical orderliness? If the question can be answered affirmatively, and there is considerable defense for it, we may then accept the shifting concept of number on utilitarian grounds. There is no better defense for any English usage than that it is useful and enhances the meaning or understanding of a sentence. The conservative Curme says, "The point of view sometimes shifts within one and the same sentence, so that the verb is now singular, now plural, although the reference in the different cases is to be the same noun," and he cites an example from *Adam Bede*: "There *was* a grand *band* hired from Rosseter, who, with *their* wonderful wind-instruments and puffed-out cheeks, *were* themselves a delightful show to the small boys." [13]

6. *Agreement with nouns of quantity.* Textbook rule: "A plural noun denoting one amount, when used as subject, takes a singular verb." [14] The same text offers the exercise "Six weeks (*does* not or *do* not) seem like a very long time in Paris" [15] In this sentence the noun *weeks* may represent one amount and take the verb *does*, or it may represent six units of time and take the plural *do*. The school child of course does not have the privilege

[13] Curme, *Syntax,* p. 51.
[14] Kimball. Book II, p. 113.
[15] *Loc. cit.*

of choice; the rule says "singular verb," and he must use a singular verb. On the same page is a still worse example of an ill-considered exercise. In the sentence, "The hat with the plumes (*cost* or *costs*) fourteen dollars" the pupil is told to choose the "correct" verb. Inasmuch as no reference to tense is made, either verb is correct, though the unfortunate student who selects *cost* (past tense) will be penalized for making *cost* (present tense plural) agree with *plumes*. In general, of course, the noun of quantity though plural in form is considered an entity and is followed by a singular verb, but where the separate parts of the total are considered individually the verb is plural. Thus we find, "Seven-eighths of the world's gold *is* in the United States," but, "Three-fourths of the people *are* starving." The verb as usual agrees with the meaning of the subject, regardless of its form.

Still another example of the faulty exercise is this: "A lot of different kinds of soft drinks (is, are) drunk in this country." [16] If the writers expect the pupils to use *is* as a verb in agreement with *lot* considered in the singular, they are running counter to standard usage which accepts *lot* with a partitive modifier as a plural; if they do expect the plural verb *are* then their exercise has no place in a consideration of number since they have provided no discussion of the use of *lot, member,* and so forth, as plurals.

The most preposterous of all textbook rules is the following: "The pronoun *I* requires the plural form of all verbs except *am,* and *was.*" [17] This rule is cited as an exception to subject-verb agreement! While it is obvious that the writer intends to show that the third person singular, present tense, of the active verb is the only

[16] Kirby and Carpenter, Book VII, p. 181.
[17] Clippinger, p. 5.

distinctly singular form of the verb, it is inconceivable that anyone would deliberately associate the idea of plurality with the singular pronoun *I*. To do so is to destroy utterly the meaning of the word *plural* and to reduce the conscientious pupil to despair. Furthermore, it displays an astounding lack of any knowledge of historical grammar on the part of the writer.

The foregoing discussion is a criticism of the inadequacy of the textbook rules for subject-verb agreement with an attempt to establish clearly two facts: first, that the rules as they appear in the textbooks are too rigid to describe past and present usage; and second, that they miss entirely the underlying principle of English concord, that the verb always agrees with the *intent* of the subject regardless of its form. Future texts must base all the rules of concord on this fundamental concept which always has been and probably always will be the actual basis for subject-verb agreement in English.

PRONOUN AGREEMENT

The pronouns *everyone, everybody, anyone, anybody,* and so forth, are regularly listed by all the textbooks as singular pronouns only; they are said to take the singular regimen wherever they are used. "For instance, *everyone, everybody, everything* seem to refer to many persons or things; but they do not mean all persons or all things taken together, but *every single, separate person* or *every single, separate thing*. These pronouns are, therefore, singular; they take singular verbs and are regarded as singular when used as antecedents."[18] As far as verb agreement is concerned the rules represent usage, for the singular verb has always been used when adjacent to these indefinite pronouns. But as antecedents of pronouns

[18] Pearson and Kirchwey, p. 330.

they have been and still are used as plural words when the sense demands a plural, despite the efforts of rule-makers to control them. In the eighteenth century there was some attempt at reducing these forms to rule with only a modicum of success. "It would not be difficult to demonstrate that the minute attention to agreement, particularly of pronouns, had little effect upon the writers of the period following. Probably quite as many cases of reference of *they* and *their* to words like *person* and *one* and *everybody* could be discovered in an equal number of pages of Jane Austin or Walter Scott and of Addison or Swift."[19] An amusing example of the uncertainty, or at least freedom from rule, prevailing in the eighteenth century is to be found in a letter from John Oldmixon in answer to Swift's letter to the Earl of Oxford, "...that everybody loves Flattery as well as himself, and Will take any Thing kindly that is said in their favour."[20]

Professor Krapp limits indefinite pronouns to use in the singular only, saying, "The pronouns each, every, either, neither, any, anyone, everyone, someone, somebody, everybody, nobody, no one, etc., are singular... and are referred to by singular pronouns."[21] On the other hand, Curme recognizes the plural usage in earlier English, and while pointing out that the singular is preferred today, agrees that the plural may also be found.[22]

When a pronoun or possessive adjective refers to a word plural in meaning, but in form being an indefinite pronoun in the singular... it was once common to indicate the plural idea by the form of the following pronoun or possessive adjective, but it is now usual to put the pronoun or possessive

[19] Leonard, *Doctrine of Correctness in English Usage, 1700-1800*, p. 225.
[20] *Loc. cit.*
[21] Krapp, *Comprehensive Guide to Good English*, p. 644.
[22] Curme, *Syntax*, p. 557.

adjective into the singular in accordance with the singular form of the antecedent: "*Nobody* knows what it is to lose a friend, till *they have* [now *he has*] lost him." (Fielding). "If the part deserved any comment, *every* considering *Christian* will make it *themselves* [now *himself*] as *they* go" [now *he goes*]. (Defoe). "I do not mean that I think *anyone* to blame for taking due care of *their* [now *his*] health." (Addison). Older usage, however, still occasionally occurs: "*Every body* is discontented with *their* [instead of *his*] lot in life." (Beaconsfield). This older literary usage survives in loose colloquial and popular speech: "Everybody has *their* [instead of *his*] faults." "It is the duty of each student to interest *themselves* [instead of *himself*] in athletics.

As an example of occasional use on the literary level today the following sentence from *Harper's* is interesting: "He had in his time been almost everybody's bosom friend, and usually *their* secretary." [23]

The Leonard-Moffett study reveals a nice distinction in the singular and plural use of the pronoun with *everyone, everybody* in two cases, one quite clear plural in meaning and the second quite clearly singular. The first sentence, "*Everyone* was here, but *they* all went home early" was placed 39 in a series of 102 items with a composite rating of 2.4 (2.0—cultivated informal English) and a rating by British linguists of 2.3. The second example, "*Everybody* brought *their* own ticket" was placed 70 in the list with a composite rating of 3.0 (halfway between acceptable and uncultivated English). It is evident from these scores by competent judges that there is a distinction in the use of *everyone* and *everybody* resting upon the implied number of the subject, regardless of rules. [24] If one may judge from current articles in the periodicals, present British usage is in-

PROBLEMS IN ENGLISH SYNTAX

clined to be more liberal toward the plural use of the indefinite pronouns than is American usage. "... there is good evidence that British usage is still equally unfettered in the matter. The great conservatism of American writers, as usual, has led them to follow this rule more carefully." [25] McKnight observes: [26]

In the use of pronouns following words or word combinations with collective meanings British use often gives a shock to an American's grammatical nerves. *"Their,"* says Richard Grant White, "is very commonly misused with reference to a singular noun." "A misuse of the word *every,*" he says is another place, "is worth remark,—the using it in a plural sense, which is very common. Thus: Every person rose and took their leave." The kinds of "misuse" here condemned in American use, in British use are established not only by long tradition but by current practice. The awkward necessity so often met with in American speech of using the double pronoun, "his or her," is obviated by the "misuse" of *their.*

This discussion is followed by a long list of examples.

The impartial student is forced to conclude that the rigid rules of the textbooks are not accurate in limiting the indefinite pronouns to singular use only. There are many occasions in English speech and writing in which the plural use is desirable for convenience, if not absolutely necessary. Less frequent, but by no means rare, examples of actual necessity occur as in "Everyone was waiting when I arrived, and *they* greeted me courteously," and "When the President left, everybody cheered; he lifted his hat in acknowledgment to *them.*" In these sentences the singular pronoun would be absurd, and there is no real occasion for revision except to avoid the

[25] Leonard, *Doctrine of Correctness in English Usage, 1700-1800,* p. 225.
[26] McKnight, "Conservatism in American Speech," p. 12.

breach of purely formal agreement.[27] It may be concluded, then, that the indefinite pronouns *everyone,*
everybody, either, neither, and so forth, when singular
in meaning are referred to by a singular pronoun; when
plural in meaning are referred to by a plural pronoun.
It must be added, however, that American usage, far
more than British usage, tends to keep these pronouns
singular whenever possible.

ADVERBIAL MODIFIERS

The position of only. The school textbooks in grammar
and composition frown upon the free position of *only* in
such sentences as: "If I *only* had five dollars!" "He *only*
wanted to speak to me." In spite of the almost universal
acceptance of these constructions in colloquial speech
and much current writing, the textbooks maintain that
unless the word *only* is in immediate juxtaposition to the
word it modifies the meaning becomes obscured or
ambiguous. Therefore they list such rules and examples
as these:

(*a*) The adverb *only* should be placed as near as possible
to the word it modifies.

WRONG: One can *only* succeed by hard work.[28]

All these rules and examples are based upon the assumption that if the word *only* is separated from the
word or phrase it modifies, some appreciable degree of
ambiguity or obscurity results. This assumption is un-

[27] Professor Leonard tells the story, "I found a remarkable instance of 'correctness' in a child's story of being ducked while in
swimming. 'When I came up, everybody was laughing at me, but
I was glad to see *him* just the same.' This was written in a seventh-
grade English class without anyone's correction or suggestion of
the form." *Doctrine of Correctness in English Usage, 1700-1800,*
p. 224, footnote.

[28] Lewis and Hosic, p. 76.

sound, for in common speech the phrase "I *only* had five dollars" is normal and is never misunderstood. In fact, should a speaker desire to limit the subject in such a sentence, he is compelled to stress the pronoun and supply a word like *alone* to be sure his meaning is clear. Similarly in the less specific uses of *only*, as in "If my vacation *only* would come!" or "If *only* John were here!" there is no feeling that the modifier limits the subject. Surely in the last sentence quoted one might expect the position of *only*, immediately preceding the subject, to lead to misunderstanding, but it is safe to assert that in all ordinary uses such a sentence is never misconstrued.

Some textbook writers feel constrained in spite of personal prejudice, to make some acknowledgment of current usage. Such statements as these may therefore be found:

(*a*) INCORRECT: I *only* wanted one but I received several. (This position for *only* is almost idiomatic in colloquial use. In writing and in formal speech, say, I wanted only one, or I wanted one only.) [29]

(*b*) English idiom seems to sanction a loose use of *only* whenever the meaning is obvious from the context.[30]

Such extreme caution as is implied in the words "almost idiomatic" and "seems to sanction" illustrates clearly the predicament of textbook grammarians confronted with the facts of usage. More adequate by far is the rule given by a textbook designed for the elementary grades: [31]

(*c*) Adverbial expressions should be so placed in the sentence as to convey just the meaning intended.

[29] John C. French, p. 110.
[30] Thomas, Manchester, and Scott, p. 163.
[31] Scott and Southworth, Book II, p. 222.

Although the examples which follow this rule indicate beyond a doubt a narrow interpretation of it, yet the rule itself is sound and is inclusive enough to satisfy the demands of current usage.

Turning now to the opinions of the authorities in usage, we find this statement by J. Lesslie Hall: [32]

The position of *only* has long been a burning question in English. Not to go farther back than fifty years, Dean Alford said in 1864 that the pedants were very strict but the language very liberal. "The adverb *only*" says he, "in many sentences where strictly speaking it ought to follow its verb, and to limit the objects of the verb, is in good English placed before the verb." "I only saw a man," he says, is our ordinary colloquial English; but the pedant should compel us to say, "I saw *only* a man." The question is the same in our day; rhetorical scholars and grammarians make their rule; the great authors, the great majority of them, are utterly oblivious of the rule and care nothing for it.

The best and most helpful statement as to *only* is found in *Mother Tongue* (III) by Gardiner, Kittredge, and Arnold. "Good usage does not fix absolutely the position of *only* with respect to the word it modifies. There is but one safe rule: Shun ambiguity. If this is observed, the pupil may feel secure."

Concerning this usage in the eighteenth century Professor Leonard says: [33]

The rules for placing modifiers were of course dictated by a general purpose of securing greater clarity; but when grammarians came to look about for actual instances, they rarely confined themselves to sentences which might actually cause difficulty or misunderstanding in their context, since such sentences are not really common in experienced writers. Instead, critics took the usual short-cut of pitching upon sentences of a fixed type regardless of their clarity or lack

[32] J. Lesslie Hall, pp. 187-189.
[33] Leonard, *Doctrine of Correctness in English Usage, 1700-1800*, p. 96.

of clarity. Sentences containing adverbs like *only* came in handy.

The only valid objection to the position of *only* in any sentence is that in that sentence its position leads to ambiguity or misunderstanding. Insomuch as in the great majority of sentences no misunderstanding occurs, the specific rules of the text are based upon a false assumption, and must be greatly revised to represent adequately current usage.

Not all. Quite in the same vein as the objections to the placing of *only* is this comment on the use of *not* with *all*. "Especial care should be taken in using the words *not* and *only*. Such a sentence as 'All students are not industrious' is sometimes used when the author intends to say 'Not all students are industrious.'"[34] The answer is that the writer knew what he was doing and deliberately used "All students are not industrious" because it is common usage in English and is not misunderstood. In fact, to express the idea of "lack of industry" as a characteristic of "all students" requires an entirely different sentence plan, for "All students are not industrious" would not convey the idea. Something like "All students are lazy" would be necessary.

Professor Leonard has a note concerning this construction in the eighteenth century.[35]

About placing *not*, the eighteenth century was quite free of formula:
> Every just observation does not occur to any one Mind. (*Reflections*, 1770, Preface, p. 10.)
> All subjects do not equally require precision. (Blair, *Lectures*, I, p. 176.)

[34] Clippinger, p. 172.
[35] Leonard, *Doctrine of Correctness in English Usage, 1700-1800*, p. 98.

All opinions are not received into the language.
(Michaelis, p. 2.)

These forms were not objected to, and seem perfectly clear.

Correlatives. The rules for the correlatives *not only ...
but also, neither ... nor, either ... or,* and so forth, spring
from a purpose identical with that for the rule about
only; namely, a desire to avoid ambiguity. But as in the
case of most rules once liberally interpreted, they have
become formal and inviolable in the current textbooks.

"Place correlatives ... next to corresponding parts of
speech. INCORRECT: I neither trusted him nor his
brother.[36] As in the case of the rules for the position of
only, these rules for the correlatives originally designed
to express a general principle of orderliness have been
copied from book to book as rigid commandments with
no effort at all to determine the nature of literary and
current practice. Hall[37] cites numerous examples from
his reading.

Professor Curme[38] cites the use of the correlative conjunctions but adds no restriction on their use. There
seems no adequate reason for requiring correlative conjunctions to be used only with parallel constructions;
current practice is endorsed by a long literary history in
allowing the free use of the correlatives when the construction employed does not obscure the intended
meaning.

So and such as intensifying adverbs. The use of the
words *so* and *such* as simple intensifying adverbs is
strongly condemned by some textbooks for all levels of
discourse, and in others is excluded from formal writing.

[36] John C. French, p. 110.
[37] J. Lesslie Hall, p. 182.
[38] Curme, *Syntax,* p. 164.

That English teachers in general follow the lead of the textbooks so far as their teaching is concerned is revealed by a ballot on usage answered by approximately 150 teachers of English in the state of Colorado. Concerning the use of *so* as an adverb, but 2 teachers allowed it to be formally correct usage, 33 acknowledged it to be fully acceptable, 94 felt that it was doubtful, and 12 condemned it utterly as illiterate.[39] The textbooks contain the following typical statements:[40]

(*a*) With the exception of *and,* there is no more abused word than *so*. Like charity, it covers a multitude of sins. There is perhaps no better place to point out the various meanings of the word and its uses, proper and improper.

So as an adverb.
PROPER: I was never so angry.

IMPROPER in formal writing: ("feminine intensive")
I was so angry! (So is used here in place of *very, exceedingly,* etc.)
Such is similarly misused. It should be followed by a clause of result introduced by *that*.

The almost universal dissemination of these rules for *so* and *such* is an interesting example of the power of literary tradition to survive in the face of literary and colloquial practice. Many of the selections of standard literature used in the classroom by the same teachers who condemn this usage contain *so* and *such* as simple intensives. Moreover, the *New English Dictionary* acknowledges this usage as follows: "*So* (14): In affirmative clauses, tending to become a mere intensive without comparative force, and sometimes emphasized in speaking and writing. Used thus by King Alfred, Gower, Dryden, Richardson, Keats, Dickens, Mrs. Gaskell, and others."

[39] Pooley, *Handbook of Current English Usage,* p. 27.
[40] Thomas, Manchester, and Scott, pp. 151, 170.

Concerning the word *so* as an adverb, Russell Thomas shows beyond all doubt that it has been used regularly by writers when a comparison is implied, even though not expressed, as in the quotations: [41]

Browning, "Pheidippides":
"Too rash
Love in its choice, paid you *so* largely service
so slack!"

Bridges, "The Garden in September":
How love *so* young could be *so* sweet.

Moreover, his examples include others from the *Blickling Homilies* to Stuart P. Sherman in which the *so* is pure intensive, with no comparison implied or expressed, as in:

Tennyson, "Tears, Idle Tears":
So sad, *so* fresh, the days that are no more.

Century Magazine, August, 1929, p. 455:
Survivors of 1865—*So* like to One Another,
So Different from Other People.

In view of so many clear examples from standard literature the positive dicta of the textbooks seem a trifle absurd. If one's taste is offended by the use of *so* as an intensive adverb he may avoid its use and deplore it in others, but there is little justification for excluding it from the usage of ordinary English.

THE DOUBLE NEGATIVE

That two negatives used in a negative predication reverse the meaning and form a positive statement is a curious tradition first enunciated by Lowth in the eighteenth century and still warmly cherished by

[41] Russell B. Thomas, pp. 557-560.

English teachers. It is all the more surprising that this conception survives with no apparent diminution in strength when one recalls the current prevalence of the phrases "can't hardly" and "can't scarcely" in the daily usage of educated people, including the majority of teachers. Sentences containing these phrases may be frowned upon by the more exacting teacher, but they are never misconstrued to be entirely affirmative; thus, "I can't hardly read this" is never interpreted as meaning, "I read this with great ease." The double negative in most cases may be fairly excluded from writing and speech of the present day on the grounds that it is out of style, currently unacceptable, but surely not on any grounds of logic or paradox. But the textbooks still adhere to the old tradition.

A person soon learns that in English two negatives coming together cancel each other. He is quickly told that to say *I didn't do nothing* does not mean what the person who says it usually means. The *not*, represented by *n't*, and the *nothing* render each other powerless. The sentence really means that the person did something and that is usually opposite to what the speaker meant. Such expressions are called double negatives.[42]

The next quotation does omit any reference to the "canceling" power of two negatives, but still fails to furnish an adequate reason for the prohibition.[43]

When the verb makes a negative assertion, it is unnecessary and incorrect to use the adjective *no* to denote the absence or lack of a quality or thing.

Of this usage Logan Pearsall Smith in his monograph *English Idioms,* says: [44]

[42] Kirby and Carpenter, Book VIII, p. 276.
[43] Pearson and Kirchwey, p. 164.
[44] Logan Pearsall Smith, p. 10.

Owing to the efforts of ... grammarians a number of English idiomatic usages have been stigmatized as incorrect, and driven from our standard speech. Of these, perhaps, the most conspicuous is the double negative, which was perfectly correct in the time of Chaucer, lingered on till the age of Shakespeare, and is still current in the speech of the vast majority of English people. Owing, however, to the logical (but most unpsychological) notion that doubling a negative destroys, instead of strengthening it, this idiom, although it was correct in Greek, and has practically reëstablished itself in French, is regarded as a gross vulgarism in modern English.

Such expressions as "I didn't get no book" and "I haven't seen nobody" may be considered entirely outside the range of acceptable current English, even though that range be liberally interpreted, but the forms "didn't hardly," "haven't scarcely," "wouldn't hardly" can less certainly be excluded. It is true that a ballot of English teachers in the state of Colorado on this usage revealed an overwhelming opinion that "haven't hardly" is definitely illiterate English. But it is also true that a large number of these teachers use the expression unconsciously in informal speech.[45]

Leonard and Moffett likewise found general disapproval in the example, "I haven't hardly any money." On a scale of 4 points, in which 1 represented literary usage, and 4 illiteracy, the general average of scores was 3.8. British judges ranked it 4.0.[46] It would seem, therefore, that "haven't hardly" has at present no standing in written English, in spite of its notably widespread use in speech.

THE SPLIT INFINITIVE

The question as to whether one may "split" an infinitive by placing an adverbial modifier between the "to" and

[45] Pooley, *Handbook of Current English Usage*, p. 39.
[46] Leonard and Moffett, p. 355.

the infinitive form of the verb has been hotly debated for a century. "Apparently, it was both a discovery and an aversion of nineteenth-century grammarians." [47] In spite of the quantities of print on the subject, and the definitive statements of linguists and grammarians, the textbooks still cleave to the nineteenth-century aversion, stating their objections with varying degrees of certainty.

A modifier should not be placed between the parts of an infinitive.
WRONG: We wished *to thoroughly explore* the cave.[48]

Do not insert an adverbial expression between the two parts of an infinitive. An occasional violation of this rule for the purpose of securing emphasis is permissible.[49]

The "occasional violators" of this rule are so numerous and so respectable and the period of their "violations" covers such a long stretch in the history of English that the rule itself becomes little more than pedantic rubbish. The vast number of examples of this usage in standard literature,[50] together with the statements of acknowledged scholars should certainly be sufficient evidence to settle this question for all time.

Otto Jespersen says of the split infinitive: [51]

... The linguistic instinct now takes *to* to belong to the preceding verb rather than to the infinitive, a fact which,

[47] Leonard, *Doctrine of Correctness in English Usage, 1700-1800*, p. 95.
[48] Clippinger, p. 172.
[49] Thomas, Manchester, and Scott, p. 535.
[50] The American authors alone include "Franklin, Freneau, Irving, Whittier, Motely, Hawthorne, Lowell, Bret Harte, H. C. Lodge, John Fiske, T. B. Aldrich, Cable, Mabie, Katherine Lee Bates, J. K. Hosmer, A. D. White, W. D. Whitney, Roosevelt, and Woodrow Wilson." From an aritcle by Wallace Rice, *The Chicago Tribune*, 1928.
[51] Jespersen, *Growth and Structure of the English Language*, p. 210.

together with other circumstances, serves to explain the phenomenon usually mistermed "the split infinitive." This name is bad because we have many infinitives without *to*. . . . Although examples of an adverb between *to* and the infinitive occur as early as the fourteenth century, they do not become very frequent until the latter half of the nineteenth century. In some cases they decidedly contribute to the clearness of the sentence by showing at once what word is qualified by the adverb.

Developing more fully this explanation of the need for the divided infinitive on the grounds of clarity and emphasis, Professor Curme writes: [52]

When the adverb precedes a verb, the verb seems more important to our feeling than the adverb even though the adverb may also be stressed. But when we are not calling attention to the verbal activity so much as to some particular in connection with it, we place the adverb expressing that particular after the verb. It is this feature that has furthered the development of the split infinitive.

J. Lesslie Hall presents an interesting comparison of rule and usage for the split infinitive in the middle of the nineteenth century.[53]

Shall an adverb be put between *to* and the other part of an infinitive? . . . This is a "burning question" and one on which verbalists disagree.

Dean Alford, in 1864, said, "Surely this is a practice entirely unknown to English speakers and writers." At this very moment Dean Alford could have found the split infinitive in the writings of Dickens, Matthew Arnold, Mrs. Gaskell, Browning, George Eliot, of his own day, Burns, Byron, Coleridge, Goldsmith, and others of earlier periods.

We must all admit, then, that the split infinitive is neither an innovation nor a vulgarism, but a rarity in pure literature; that it is very clear and very convenient and has a right to a trial in the language.

[52] Curme, "The Split Infinitive," p. 341.
[53] J. Lesslie Hall, pp. 266-271.

The root-infinitive usually has before it the preposition *to,* which is called its sign, and is to be considered and described as a part of it. In the oldest English, this preposition was only used with the infinitive when it had a real prepositional value. . . .

The discussion of the uses of the adverb in infinitive constructions can find no better lead than that offered by Professor Curme. When the verbal force of the infinitive is strongly felt, its adverbial modifiers are naturally placed as they would be in a sentence in which the verb is strongly stressed (as in the phrase "strongly stressed" just preceding). When the adverb is the more important feature it tends to follow the verb (as in "it is stressed strongly"). It is only natural and idiomatic, therefore, to find in sentences in which the infinitive has an actual verbal force one or more adverbial modifiers preceding it. The following sentences illustrate the point well: "He stood high in the colony, was extravagant and fond of display, and, his fortune being jeopardized, he hoped to *more than retrieve* it by going into speculations in western lands." (Theodore Roosevelt, *The Winning of the West,* Vol I, Ch. II.) "To an active mind it may be easier to bear along all the qualifications of an idea than to *first imperfectly conceive* such an idea." (Herbert Spencer, *Philosophy of Style.*) "When I hear gentlemen say that politics ought to let business alone, I feel like inviting them to *first consider* whether business is letting politics alone." (Woodrow Wilson, February 24, 1912.)[54]

In view of the overwhelming evidence in support of the split infinitive it seems not unreasonable to expect the school-books to refrain from prohibiting it at least, and better still, to give some adequate description of its

[54] I am indebted to Professor Curme, "The Split Infinitive," p. 341, for these illustrations.

use. The following is a suggestion: the adverbial modifier of an infinitive may be placed between the parts of the infinitive as in "to steadily labor" or immediately following it, as in "to labor steadily." When the adverbial modifier is short and is less emphatic than the verbal force of the infinitive, it is usually placed between the *to* and the rest of the infinitive: "He worked silently and swiftly, hoping *to speedily end* his patient's discomfort." When the adverbial modifier is long, or is more emphatic than the verbal force of the infinitive, it is usually placed after it: "He came to expect *ever more and more* a change in his too even life"; "I want you to come *quickly*." Occasionally the adverb precedes the infinitive. Many stylists avoid splitting the infinitive as a mark of elegance, but usage has established it beyond any doubt.

The discussion of the split infinitive raises two other interesting questions. Is the *to* a necessary part of the infinitive? May the *to* stand alone in place of a previously expressed infinitive?

Concerning the first question, Whitney says: [55]

> The root-infinitive usually has before it the preposition *to*, which is called its sign, and is to be considered and described as a part of it. In the oldest English, this preposition was only used with the infinitive when it had a real prepositional value. . . .
> But the *to* is also in a great many cases omitted.
> *a.* After verbs generally used as auxiliaries: *do, will, shall, may, can,* and *must*
> *b.* After a few other verbs, either usually or optionally: *dare, help, need, 'gin* (for begin); and *please* and *go* in certain uses
> *c.* In certain peculiar or elliptical constructions: *had* followed by *lief, rather*; in comparative phrases, like *as well yield at once as struggle vainly*; after *but* following a negative; thus, *she cannot but grieve for him*

[55] Whitney, *Essentials of English Grammar,* p. 212.

d. After certain verbs, when preceded by a word having the relation of object to those verbs, but also the logical value of a subject to the infinitive: *see, hear, feel, let, make, bid, help, have* (in the sense of "make" or "cause"), *know, find*

With so many uses of the root infinitive without the preposition *to,* we are prepared for the definite statement of *The New Century Dictionary* under the discussion of *to* with the infinitive, "The preposition is no part of the verb." It is consistent with the idiom of English to find groups of infinitives introduced by a single *to,* as in Shakespeare's "To shake the head, relent, and sigh, and yield." and in the common phrases, "To come and go," "to do or die," "to win or lose." With these examples in mind there seems no reasonable objection to such sentences as: "He determined to enter and win the race"; "She refused to eat, talk, or move." The use of the infinitive in compound relationships such as these has led to a still further development in such phrases as "try and do it," "come and see me" which are considered problems of usage rather than syntax and are therefore discussed in the next chapter.[56] Leaving out of consideration for the moment this last use of the infinitive, it may be justly concluded that the preposition *to* may introduce a group of infinitives without being repeated before each one of them.

On the other hand, may the *to* be used alone to represent an infinitive previously expressed or understood as in the sentence "I ought to go, but I don't want *to* (go)"? Dean Alford said in 1864, "It seems to me, that we ever regard the 'to' of the infinitive as inseparable from the verb." One text also objects to this construction with the words, "In writing, *to* alone should not be used

[56] See pp. 132, 133.

in place of an infinitive: 'Do as I told you *to*.'" [57] It has already been shown that Dean Alford was wrong with regard to the *to* introducing more than one infinitive; in the examples given above the *to* was entirely separable from the verb. It remains to show that he was also wrong with respect to the *to* substituted for the verb. Whitney says, "The infinitive or the participle of a repeated verb-phrase is very often omitted and the auxiliary left alone to represent the phrase; ... In easy colloquial speech even a repeated infinitive is represented by its sign *to* alone." [58]

Professor Jespersen gives the example "Will you come? I should like *to*," and calls this use of the word *to* a *pro-infinitive* on the analogy of the pronoun.[59] In a later amplification he adds, "in the same way in colloquial English we may have an isolated *to* standing as a representative of an infinitive with *to*: *I told them to* (I told them to run). Psychologically these are cases of aposiopesis ('stop-short sentences' or 'pull-up sentences') ... the infinitive is left out as in (Will you play?) *Yes, I will,* or *Yes I am going to* (*I am willing to, anxious to*)." [60]

There seems to be no doubt as to the complete independence of the preposition *to* and the root infinitive. Either the root infinitive may stand alone, not only with certain verbs but in groups of infinitives introduced by an initial *to*, or the *to* itself may stand alone as the sign of a previously expressed or implied infinitive. The "inseparability" of which Dean Alford wrote simply does not exist, and certainly cannot be advanced as an argument against the "splitting" of the infinitive.

[57] Scott and Southworth, Book II, p. 213.
[58] Whitney, p. 242.
[59] Jespersen, *Philosophy of Grammar*, p. 82.
[60] *Ibid.,* p. 142.

THE DANGLING PARTICIPLE AND GERUND

Writers of textbooks, especially those of high-school and college level, agree quite generally that the participial or gerund construction at the beginning of the sentence must be followed closely by the subject of the sentence; that the subject must be expressed, and that the relationship between the verbal modifier and the subject must be clear and unambiguous. Failure to observe these rules of syntax results in a misrelated or "dangling" construction of a particularly heinous nature, always avoided by careful writers and righteously condemned by grammarians. Two examples from textbooks will serve to show the nature of the rules:

(*a*) A participle or a gerund phrase is correctly used, generally speaking, only
    (1) When the noun or pronoun which it modifies, or which represents the agent or recipient of the action that it expresses, is explicitly present in the sentence; and
    (2) When the parts of the sentence in which it appears are so ordered that the reader unconsciously connects it with the appropriate noun or pronoun.[61]

(*b*) A participle that has no noun or pronoun to modify is called a *loose,* or *dangling, participle.* "Loose" participles show loose and careless thinking. Avoid them and be careful not only to express the noun or the pronoun that the participle modifies, but also to place the participle so near this word that there can be no mistake as to the meaning.[62]

It is granted at the outset of this discussion that the misrelated participle or gerund frequently produces an effect distressing to the orderly mind; the meaning is not

---

[61] Thomas, Manchester, and Scott, p. 164.
[62] Pearson and Kirchwey, p. 394.

only distorted but is sometimes rendered utterly ludi-
crous. No student once having read or heard such sentences as, "While engaged in a delicate piece of crochet-
ing, an elephant passed our house," or "Having eaten
our lunch, the car pushed its way through the tortuous
canyon," would be apt to commit so obvious a fault;
these sentences he recognized as "howlers," subject to
ridicule.[63] But much less obvious is such a sentence as
this: "Having looked at our watches, no time was lost in
getting started on our way." The formalist can insist that
"time" is the subject of the verbal phrase "having looked
at our watches," but in actual speech does anyone mis-
construe such a sentence? In writing, it is true, under
cold and deliberate scrutiny this sentence incurs censure,
but is it misunderstood? Is it not a certain feeling for
syntactical orderliness rather than misunderstanding of
the author's meaning which prompts criticism of such a
sentence? And furthermore, if the meaning is so clear
that the sense of orderliness is lulled by the felicitous
expression of the idea, do not even careful writers under
such circumstances violate the rules for participial and
gerund constructions? The last question can be answered
affirmatively from overwhelming evidence.

J. Lesslie Hall says, "This construction is condemned in
practically all the textbooks on grammar and rhetoric."
After a discussion of the rules as they appear in the textbooks, and a comment on the verdict of Professor Krapp,
which is treated more fully below, he continues: [64]

Let us see, then, what a disinterested foreigner says about
it. . . . We refer to Mätzner, the eminent grammarian. Of this

---

[63] Professor W. E. Leonard furnishes another example from one
of his freshman themes of an earlier date: "Going up the hill, the
statue of Lincoln struck my eye."

[64] J. Lesslie Hall, pp. 167, 168.

participle he says, 'Although the participle in general, where it stands absolutely, is not without a substantive or pronoun on which it has to lean, participles standing alone also occur, which lean in part mediately upon a noun, or leave to be supplied a notion already named; but, in part, completely isolated, must have a subject to be conjectured.' This scholar, then, recognizes the participle standing alone.

Hall also presents a list from his own reading, showing 189 instances of the isolated participle or gerund in 68 authorities from Latimer to Stevenson. In conclusion he says: [65]

The "misrelated participle" goes back to the Anglo-Saxon period. It is found both in prose and in poetry. It comes out clearly in Mandeville and Chaucer. . . . It is seen in the Mystery Plays, Latimer, Shakespeare, and in every decade down to the present day. It is used in polite society and by cultivated speakers without number. Certainly it may be called the "misapprehended," the "persecuted" participle.

Professor Krapp states the general rule, but adds a note indicating that its observance is not universal.[66]

A modifying word or phrase must be used in such a way as to make clear the syntactical relationship of the word or phrase to the part of the sentence which it modifies. Thus a present participle should not be used without a word to which it may be attached, as in *Examining the box, the money was found untouched.* But this rule is not invariably observed even by good writers, as in *Thence, looking up and however far, each fir stands separate against the sky no bigger than an eyelash* (Stevenson, *Silverado Squatters*).

But Professor Krapp himself writes, "Looking back there to the primitive psychology of human speech, what are the evidences with respect to this notion of original simplicity and orderliness?" [67] In this sentence by an

[65] *Ibid.,* p. 170.
[66] Krapp, *Comprehensive Guide to Good English,* p. 647.
[67] Krapp, *The Knowledge of English,* p. 37.

eminent scholar the isolated syntax of the participle *looking* is apparently not felt to be improper usage, even though it is used "without a word to which it may be attached."

A more recent study [68] is devoted to a comparison of the rules of contemporary textbook writers with their own usage regarding the misrelated constructions. Quoting rules (for the dangling participle) from a dozen or more texts, the author displays in each case sentences from the same or another work by the same writer in which he has unconsciously used the isolated participle. Similarly, and with even more instances, he shows that the dangling gerund is frequent in the writings of those who oppose it by formal rules. Quite properly he says, "My object in bringing to light some discrepancies between canon and practice is not to reveal that rhetoricians slip occasionally; for to my mind their supposed slips are not slips at all. Rather my object is to show that the very discrepancies prove the rules unwarranted, and that therefore breaches of these rules cannot properly be regarded as errors." [69] And in conclusion, "After carefully weighing all the facts, my inference is that the rules forbidding these locutions are decidedly weak." [70]

Professor Curme, on the other hand, sides with the rulemakers. He says: [71]

In general, however, although occasionally found in good authors it is felt as slovenly English in spite of its frequency in colloquial speech: "*Being not yet fully grown,* his trousers were too long." In older English, the dangling participle was more widely used than today. It was employed even by careful writers where it cannot now be used: "In their meals there

[68] Steinbach, "The Misrelated Constructions," pp. 181-197.
[69] *Ibid.,* p. 181.
[70] *Ibid.,* p. 196.
[71] Curme, *Syntax,* p. 160.

is great silence and grauitie, *using* wine rather to ease the stomacke then (now *than*) to load it." (John Lyly, *Euphues and His England,* Works, II, p. 194, A. D. 1580.)

There is sufficient evidence to take exception to Professor Curme's statement in three points: first, that the use of the dangling construction is "occasional" in literature; second, that "it is felt as slovenly English; and third, that it was used in the past "where it cannot now be used." J. Lesslie Hall has shown that this construction is widely found in literature throughout the history of English; it is easier to find examples of it than to find examples of almost any other disputed usage. He quotes Professor O. F. Emerson as saying, "This is the misrelated participle occasionally found in modern English," but a glance at the table reveals that Professor Emerson himself contributed three of the examples used by Hall.[72] The word "occasional" cannot be used accurately in describing the frequency of this usage.

To the charge that it is felt to be "slovenly English" we must answer it is felt so in theory, but not in practice. Steinbach has shown that the leading college grammarians steadfastly propose rules for the dangling constructions which they themselves do not observe in writing. Moreover, he adds a list of distinguished students of language who have not felt, in their own writings, that they were guilty of "slovenly English" in employing an isolated participle or gerund. The list includes (with the date of the work in which the example was found): G. P. Marsh, 1862; John Earle, 1890; Barrett Wendel, 1893; T. R. Lounsbury, 1908; George Saintsbury, 1912; W. T. Brewster, 1913; F. H. Vizetelly, 1915; Robert Bridges, 1921; L. P. Smith, 1923.[73] Examples

[72] J. Lesslie Hall, p. 170.
[73] Steinbach, p. 195.

taken from the published works of men of such caliber cannot be branded "slovenly English."

It is a little more difficult to answer exactly the third proposition, that the dangling constructions cannot be used today as they once were, inasmuch as Professor Curme offers but one example. Moreover, in the example he offers, the construction which is no longer acceptable is not the dangling participle, but rather the adjective clause modifying a possessive pronoun *their*. No one today may say, "At their banquet there was wine, who seldom touch anything but water." We may agree with Professor Curme that the sentence he offers is out of accord with present-day syntax, but not because of the dangling construction. The type of modification used by Lyly is no longer acceptable, and for that reason the dangling modifier "is employed where it cannot now be used." On the other hand, there are abundant examples from current literature to prove that wherever the mis-related participle was used without obscurity in the past it may be used today with equal clarity.[74]

After all, although the textbooks fail to observe the fact, the dangling constructions are a form of ellipsis. Like all other ellipses they are good when the meaning is clear, but bad when the meaning is obscured. When Robert Bridges writes, "In talking with friends the common pleas...,"[75] he means of course, "In talking with friends, *I learn* that the common plea...." or "*I am told* that...." No one could possibly mistake his meaning. Rather he is employing a commendable and useful abbreviation in which the construction "In talking with friends" is fully equivalent to "When I am talking to

[74] As for example, "Musing by night on thee, this fancy came." William Ellery Leonard, *Sonnets on Shakespeare.*
[75] Bridges, p. 22.

friends, I learn...." The omitted clause is no more necessary here than in "I am as tall as she *is tall*," where the
complementary clause is always omitted. No general rule
can be advanced to cover all cases; each use must rest
upon its fitness and clearness in the sentence.

The textbooks, therefore, must modify their rules considerably. They must point out that although the initial
participial or gerund phrase is frequently followed by
an expressed subject, the subject can be and frequently
is omitted when the meaning is not obscured. They must
show by examples when the subject may or may not be
omitted. And most of all they must cease to brand the
usage in its legitimate functions as "slovenly English,"
"improper usage," or as a sign of "loose and careless
thinking."

THE CASE OF THE NOUN OR PRONOUN WITH GERUND

There is considerable uncertainty and doubt at the
present time concerning the correct case of the noun or
the pronoun preceding a gerund. A recent letter of en-
quiry puts the problem clearly. Quoting the sentence in
question, "I discovered when selling hose of the old construction why cities had to replenish it so often and I
laid (*sic!*) awake nights trying to find a remedy to
prevent the cracking of the rubber by reason of *it* being
necessary to carry the hose flattened," the writer says,
"Our proof-reader changed the second 'it' to read 'its,'
having the rule in mind that the substantive modifying
a gerund should be in the possessive case (Woolley, 1909
edition, p. 18.)" [76] The rule here referred to appears in
various forms in the current textbooks.

It is clear from these rules that the textbooks favor the

[76] Quoted from a letter to the author from Low's Letter Service,
Chicago, Illinois.

possessive case for the substantive modifying a gerund, particularly when it is a pronoun. Oddly enough in the eighteenth century there were vigorous denunciations of the possessive case in this construction, the objective being preferred.

The first comment on this construction is a severe reprobation by George Harris, the author of the *Observations*: "Another instance in which *s* is used as an abbreviation without the least pretence for it:...Doctrine of a future STATE'S being taught;...equity of the Episcopal CHURCH'S being. ..." Lowth...spoke of expressions like "the Rules' being observed..." and "its being disregarded" as "anomalies to be rooted out." Priestly admits either possessive or accusative with the gerund....Campbell...concludes formally "that the idiom in question ought not to be entirely repudiated." Baker first stated a positive rule...; Webster is equally positive on his point, and we perhaps owe to him the dogma that the possessive must invariably be used in this construction.[77]

In the nineteenth century, although the rule was becoming quite firmly established in favor of the possessive case through the influence of Webster and his followers, Whitney wrote in his grammar: [78]

...the two constructions, of an objective case qualified by a present participle and of a possessive qualifying an infinitive in *ing*, are to a certain extent interchangeable; and the question sometimes arises as to which should be preferred. There are cases where both are equally proper; but even among good writers (and yet more among careless ones), the one is occasionally found where more approved usage would favor the other: thus,

> pardon me blushing
> the certainty of the old man interrupting him
> the hope of society is in men caring for other things;

[77] Leonard, *Doctrine of Correctness in English Usage, 1700-1800*, pp. 199, 200.

[78] Whitney, *Essentials of English Grammar*, p. 223.

Where *my blushing, the old man's interrupting him,* and *men's caring* would doubtless be better.

Whitney recognizes the two uses; he admits the possibility of either being (*sic!*) correct in a certain context, and he gives as the only basis for the selection of the customary usage his feeling for what was approved in his day. There is little doubt that "me blushing" is a rare and unusual construction, chiefly objectionable because it attracts attention to itself; the other two examples, "the old man interrupting him" and "men caring" are by no means unusual and have considerable literary backing. Jespersen says: [79]

I ... here content myself with quoting a few sentences of the new construction out of several hundreds which I have collected: "When we talk of this man or that woman being no longer the same person" (Thackeray), "Besides the fact of those three being there, the drawbridge is kept up" (A. Hope), "When I think of this being the last time of seeing you" (Miss Austen), "The possibility of such an effect being wrought by such a cause" (Dickens), "He insisted upon the chamber carrying out his policy" (Lecky), "I have not the least objection in life to a rogue being hung" (Thackeray), "No man ever heard of opium leading into delirium tremens" (DeQuincey), "The suffering arises simply from people not understanding this truism" (Ruskin).

This last example from Ruskin is identical in form with Whitney's last example, "The hope of society is in men caring for other things," of which he says *"men's caring* would doubtless be better." It is not unreasonable to conclude that Whitney in making this statement was expressing the nineteenth-century preference for the possessive case without being fully aware of the extent to which the objective case was employed by writers of repute. Jespersen concludes, "These examples will show

[79] Jespersen, *Growth and Structure of the English Language,* pp. 200, 201.

that the construction is especially useful in those cases where for some reason or other it is impossible to use the genitive case, but that it is also found where no such reason could be adduced." [80]

In modern usage there can be recognized four distinct situations in which the choice of the objective or possessive case of the substantive is governed in part by custom, and in part by the exigencies of the construction. That no general rule can cover the uses of the substantive with the gerund should be clear from the enumeration below.

1. *The pronoun immediately preceding the gerund.* Example: "Do you object to his joining us?" Ordinarily the possessive case is employed in this construction and may be considered standard. J. Lesslie Hall says of this use, "Pronouns . . . are nearly always genitive in reputable authors." [81] Despite this general use of the possessive, there are cases in speech at least in which the objective is used for special emphasis in sentences where the pronoun is the focus point of attention in the phrase. Such cases are, "What do you think of *him* being elected?" "Can you picture *me* jumping rope?" The objective case here is clearly a device for emphasis, for the force of the reference to the person represented by the pronoun would be lost in "his being elected," "my jumping rope." For this case then the statement of a rule should be: The pronoun immediately preceding a gerund is usually in the possessive case, except that in sentences where great emphasis on the pronoun is desired the objective case may be used.

When *this* or *that* precede the gerund as in the sentence "Why do you insist on *this* (or *that*) being done?"

[80] *Loc. cit.*
[81] J. Lesslie Hall, p. 138.

the possessive forms would be so odd as to arouse wonder and are virtually never used. George Harris wrote
in 1752, "*This's being done* would mark a man of no
education."[82] J. Lesslie Hall also notes these words as
"cases in which the possessive is rarely used."[83]

2. *The pronoun separated from the gerund by a
modifying phrase or clause.* Example: "Have you heard
of his, the thief's, being captured?" This is a very rare construction and probably is found only in informal speech
in cases where the antecedent of the pronoun is not clear
from the preceding context. It is governed by the same
rule as case 1.

3. *The noun immediately preceding the gerund.* Example: "I never heard of a woman (or woman's) being
offended by flattery." It is about this case that the controversy rages, and may long continue to do so since the
literary and current usage is evenly divided. J. Lesslie
Hall presents a list of 53 authorities, including 217 cases,
from the Rolls of Parliament, 1435-1437, to Sir Henry
Taylor, who used the objective case (without *'s*) of the
noun before the gerund. But a similar list of 54 authorities, including 231 cases, from Milton to Huxley shows
that the genitive (with *'s*) is quite as widely used. He
concludes with,[84]

> Some interesting deductions can be drawn from the fore-
> going statistics:
> (1) The form without *'s* is older than the other, as we
> have already seen from the authorities.
> (2) The two forms are about numerically even (231 to
> 217) in the literature read.
> (3) Both forms are used by a large number of au-
> thors. . . .

[82] Leonard, *Doctrine of Correctness in English Usage, 1700-1800,*
p. 126.
[83] J. Lesslie Hall, p. 141.
[84] J. Lesslie Hall, pp. 138-141.

(4) The objective form is much stronger than the other in some of the best recent writers....

Jespersen says that the objective *-ing* is two hundred years old; but the table proves that it goes back to 1435-1437, showing itself later in the writings of Sir Thomas More. It comes out pretty strongly in Daniel DeFoe, who, in the tables, has nine objectives and four genitives. A hundred years later Boswell uses the objective pretty frequently, though preferring the genitive.

In the Leonard-Moffett study the sentence "What was the reason for *Bennett making* that disturbance?" was ranked number 35 in a list of 102 items, with a general average rating of 2.5 on a scale of 4 points. The British linguists rated it 2.1, showing as usual greater liberality in points of divided usage.[85]

Professor Krapp says, "A noun or a pronoun modifying a gerund is by rule in the possessive case. . . . But this rule frequently fails of observance, both in written and in spoken English. It is most likely to be observed when the word before the gerund names a person. . . ."[86] This last statement of Professor Krapp's is surely open to question, inasmuch as a random collection of examples, like that of Hall for example, contains a fair number of proper nouns as well as common nouns. " . . . it does not appear that *Smith's* is to any extent more general than *barn's* in the model sentences at the head of this section,"[87] he concludes.

It appears then, that a rule for this third case should read: A noun immediately preceding a gerund may take the possessive or the objective case. Both have adequate literary authority, with a tendency toward the objective case appearing in recent writers.

[85] Leonard and Moffett, p. 345.
[86] Krapp, *Comprehensive Guide to Good English,* p. 643.
[87] J. Lesslie Hall, p. 143.

4. *The noun separated from the gerund by a modifying phrase or clause.* Examples: "Have you heard of old Smith, the police chief, being retired?" "I have been told recently of the lad, who was always a poor rider, taking a serious tumble." That this case applies more to the proper noun than the common noun seems reasonable from the fact that the proper noun more frequently needs an appositional or non-restrictive modifier than does the common noun. J. Lesslie Hall is the only writer who calls attention to this case saying, "When modifying words, phrases, or clauses intervene between the noun and the *-ing* form . . . in none of these sentences can the *'s* be used."[88] For the fourth case the rule must apparently be: When the noun is separated from the gerund by a modifying phrase or clause, it always takes the objective case.

In summary, it is clear from the evidence that no single rule such as, "The infinitive in *-ing* takes a possessive noun or pronoun," can adequately describe the substantive with the gerund. We have seen that there are two cases in which the possessive case is generally preferred, although for reasons of emphasis the objective may be used; a third situation in which the objective and possessive cases have equal authority and frequency; and a fourth instance in which the objective is invariably employed. The textbooks must be cognizant of all these situations in order to describe adequately the usage of the substantive with the gerund.

THE COMPARISON OF ADJECTIVES

The rather common practice of using the superlative degree of the adjective when speaking of two persons or things (sometimes described as the "careless" practice)

[88] J. Lesslie Hall, p. 141.

is uniformly condemned by the school and college text-books in English. "When comparing *two* objects use the comparative degree (never the superlative)." [89] The rules of the other texts are similar. Yet despite these rules the use of the superlative is very common in speech and is by no means unknown in writing. Hall says, "Polite conversation teems with this locution; in fact, only the most careful confine themselves to the other. Indeed, it would seem that the comparative degree of adjectives is on the road to extinction except before *than*." [90] While this view may be a trifle extreme, there is sound literary authority as well as current usage to defend the free use of the superlative.

From Professor Leonard we learn that [91]

No one in the eighteenth century seems to have taken as a serious anomaly the use of the superlative for comparing two persons or things. Priestly says it is "very common" and "very pardonable." Campbell concludes, "We say rightly, 'This is the weaker of the two, or ... the weakest of the two.' " ... Webster, in speaking of the "strongest of the two" as "not so correct as stronger" close to the place where he himself uses a superlative in this fashion, is probably to be understood as satisfying only the decent claims of reason and analogy. Certainly nobody in the eighteenth century, so far as it was here explored, took this matter as a serious and irrefragable rule.

Whitney observes the great frequency in the use of the superlative with two: "The comparative degree strictly implies a comparison between two objects, the superlative between more than two. Yet ... both in ordinary talk and in literature, it is very common to speak of one of two things as being *the longest*, although to say

[89] Raymond, p. 198.
[90] J. Lesslie Hall, p. 280.
[91] Leonard, *Doctrine of Correctness in English Usage, 1700-1800*, pp. 61, 75.

the longer is more accurate and more approved." [92] Professor Lounsbury also defends the superlative, saying that it is "met with constantly in the best writers." [93] Curme notes that the superlative of *two* " . . . still survives in popular and colloquial speech, as in 'the *smallest* of the two.' Sometimes in the literary language: 'They (i.e., the two squirrels) seemed to vie with one another who should be *most bold*.' (Thoreau)" [94]

From the statements and examples cited above it seems fair to conclude that the textbook rule, "When comparing *two* objects use the comparative degree (never the superlative)" is inaccurate with regard to current usage. The superlative is sometimes used, not only in colloquial speech where it is quite common, but in the published work of careful writers. Jespersen notes that "apart from set phrases like the *lower lip* and the *upper end* the natural tendency in modern English is to use the superlative everywhere." [95] At any rate, we may conclude that the superlative of two is neither inaccurate nor incorrect.

May such "perfect" or "complete" adjectives as *dead, square, round, equal, circular,* and so forth, be compared? The textbooks declare vehemently that they may not be compared, in words similar to these: "A few adjectives denote qualities that cannot exist in different degrees and hence they can neither be compared nor modified by *more* and *most*." [96] (QUERY: Is not modification by *more* and *most* regular English comparison?) But the frequent appearance of such phrases as "more dead than alive" "become more equal" "squarer than" "rounder than" and

[92] Whitney, *Essentials of English Grammar,* p. 81.
[93] Lounsbury, *History of the English Language,* p. 252.
[94] Curme, *Syntax,* p. 504.
[95] Jespersen, *Growth and Structure of the English Language,* p. 250.
[96] Scott and Southworth, Book II, p. 151.

so forth, leads one to suspect that these adjectives are
compared regularly in colloquial speech and at least
sometimes in writing.

In the eighteenth century "The comparison of sup-
posedly incomparable adjectives like *chief, extreme,
round, perfect,* 'already superlative in signification,' was
seriously debated. . . . Lowth admits that 'poetry is in
possession of these . . . improper superlatives, and may be
indulged in the use of them' . . . but even this divagation
from strict logic was the subject of serious concern." [97]

From his reading Hall reports a number of instances
of these "improper comparatives and superlatives." [98]

The present writer has seen the following cases: *Chiefest,*
seven times in the King James Bible; four times in Shakespeare, once in Marlowe, Jeremy Taylor, Butler, Swift, Lamb,
Emerson, Dean Trench, Phoebe Cary, Saintsbury, and Tennyson. *More perfect,* once in the Bible. *Most unique,* once in
Dr. Henry Van Dyke. *Most favorite,* once each in Dr. Johnson, Irving, and Professor William Minto. *Most principal,*
once in the Prayer Book. *Very unanimous,* twice in Bishop
Burnet. *Deadest,* once each in Emerson and Browning. *Cor-
rectest,* once in Lamb. *Extremest,* twice in Congreve. *Most
excellent* and *more excellent* are found in the Bible; the former
certainly has wide vogue in polite society. *Very excellent*
comes out prominently in one classic passage in the Prayer
Book Psalter.

It may be contended by some that since these examples are drawn so largely from the diction of an older age,
or from poetic diction in the present, they do not give
authority to the use of *more round, most exact, whiter,*
and so forth, in modern English prose. But such eminent
contemporary scholars as Lounsbury, Kittredge, and
Curme all defend the usage. The latter says, "While we

[97] Leonard, *Doctrine of Correctness in English Usage, 1700-1800,*
p. 113.
[98] J. Lesslie Hall, pp. 28, 29.

today in general avoid pleonastic comparisons, we do not feel such forms as *more perfect, most perfect, deader, deadest, more unique,* etc. as pleonastic, since we have in mind degrees of approach to something perfect, dead, or unique." [99] It seems almost beyond doubt that with regard to the comparison of "complete" adjectives, the textbooks are still voicing the "serious concern" of the eighteenth century, in ignorance of, or in spite of, the accepted usage in literature, early and current, the decisions of eminent linguists, and the language habits of members of polite society. A language rule opposed to such authority becomes futile and ridiculous.

THE INDEFINITE *It*

The rules restricting the use of *it* are harmfully misleading to the inexperienced student. Such a rule as, "Do not use *it* without an antecedent except in impersonal expressions such as *it seems, it snows, it is warm,*" [100] arbitrarily cuts out many common and useful constructions with *it* which may not be strictly included under the term "impersonal" as illustrated by the examples accompanying the rule. For example, the following rule from a widely used text seems to contradict in practice what it and the rule above express in theory. "A pronoun should refer definitely to its antecedent. *It* is not enough that there should be a specific antecedent for a pronoun. The reference should be so explicit that no confusion is possible." [101] The word beginning the second sentence is clearly an *it* without an antecedent, either specific or general, and it is not part of an impersonal expression like "it is warm" or "it rains." Just exactly what is *it*, if

[99] Curme, *Syntax,* p. 504.
[100] Raymond, p. 459.
[101] Thomas, Manchester, and Scott, p. 168.

not a pronoun without an antecedent conventionally used with an accepted type of syntax? The point to be stressed here is not that the rule-makers violated their own rule, although if their statements are to be taken literally such is the case; but rather that *it* is frequently used without a definite antecedent in constructions other than "it rains," "it is warm," and is so commonly accepted in these constructions that careful rule-makers could use it unwittingly in the heart of a general rule prohibiting it!

In point of fact, the use of *it* without an antecedent is a useful and respectable construction in modern English, having roots far back in the history of English. Professor Curme recognizes three distinct uses fully established in English which he treats of at some length.

SITUATION "IT" AS SUBJECT. *It* is much used as subject to point to a person or thing that is at first presented in only dim outlines by the situation, but is often later identified by a predicate noun: *"It's John, or Anna, or the boys."* ... *It* is often a substitute for a noun obvious from the situation or the context: *"It* is twenty miles to Chicago." [102] [This use of the pronoun *it* without an antecedent is exceedingly common in spoken and written English and must be acknowledged to be standard English by the most discriminating grammarian.]

IMPERSONAL "IT." We now say, *"It* rained yesterday," but in Gothic ... there was no *it* here. The verb had no subject at all. ... This *it*, though containing no real meaning, serves the useful purpose of giving the statement the outward form of an ordinary declarative sentence with an expressed subject, thus making it possible to preserve under changed conditions a useful old construction perfectly intact. ... [103] [Since this usage is recognized by the textbooks, no further elaboration is here necessary.]

ANTICIPATORY "IT." When we desire to call especial attention to the subject, we often withhold it for a time, causing

[102] Curme, *Syntax*, p. 7.
[103] *Ibid.*, pp. 7-8.

the feeling of suspense. "*It* is useless, of no use, no use, no good *your saying anything*." ... Anticipatory *it* is also used to point to a following subject *that* clause or a subject infinitive clause. "*It* is necessary *that you exert yourself*" (or *to exert yourself*)....Anticipatory *it* is also used when it is desired to emphasize a predicate adjective or noun, provided, however, that the logical subject is a singular noun denoting a lifeless thing, or is a clause.... After the analogy of the emphatic predicate adjectives and nouns ... it has become common to make any noun, adverb, or adverbial phrase or clause emphatic by converting it into an emphatic predicate introduced by *it is* (or *was*) and followed by the subject of the sentence in the form of a subject clause.[104] Here is an abundance of uses for the indefinite *it* not included in the purely impersonal category, which are all recognized and acceptable usages. To this list might be added another, the *it* in the sentences, "He hoofed *it* home," "We footed *it* across the fields," in which the *it* may be described as an indefinite object. The word *it* without any antecedent sometimes follows an intransitive verb as if it were an object. ... It might be regarded as a part of the verb itself.[105]

It is of course quite evident that the authors of the rule, "A pronoun should refer definitely to its antecedent," did not have in mind, or purposely overlooked the uses of the indefinite *it* as a matter apart from the rule they were propounding. The only criticism which can justly be upheld against this rule is that it is too general in its wording and might thereby seriously mislead an inexperienced teacher or literal-minded student. But with respect to the rule, "Do not use *it* without an antecedent except in impersonal expressions," very severe criticism is in order. Surely a textbook rule which arbitrarily excludes five or six standard literary uses of the word *it* must be an indication of unjustifiable oversight on the part of the authors, or else must imply that they gave a much wider

[104] *Ibid.*, pp. 11, 12.
[105] Cross, p. 390.

interpretation to the word *impersonal* than is found in their own examples or in the examples of other textbooks.

The sentence, "When a pupil does poor work, it is not always the fault of the teacher," is condemned on the grounds that *it* has no specific antecedent. Nevertheless there is considerable defense for this construction, which is by no means rare in current usage, on the basis that any word other than *it* requires an awkward shift of subject conveniently avoided by the use of *it*. Thus, "When a pupil does poor work, the teacher is not always at fault," or, "When a pupil does poor work, the fault is not always the teacher's," in either case the subject shifts from *pupil* to *teacher* or to *fault*, whereas the *it* retains the subject idea "pupil's work" throughout the sentence. Though grammatically anomalous this construction is both useful and prevalent.

VIII

Problems in English Word Choice

The materials considered in this chapter are rather miscellaneous in character and have, therefore, not been organized into specific categories. Inasmuch as they are frequently dealt with in grammars and handbooks under the actual word concerned, as for example *sit* and *set, if* or *whether,* they are arranged in this chapter in alphabetical order for easy reference. It may be objected that some items found here are more properly grammar or syntax than mere usage, and should be placed in the preceding chapters. If there be such, the reader's leniency is asked toward the application of the term "usage" to this section. It is taken here to include all those items of English speech which are considered chiefly on the grounds of propriety rather than on the grounds of grammatical accuracy or syntactical orderliness. Thus the word *set* as applied to a "setting hen" is questioned by formalists not so much because it is a transitive verb transferred to an intransitive function as it is rebuked by them for being a vulgar or dialect use. With this interpretation of the term "usage" it is believed that the following items are consistent.

A great deal of interesting material has been excluded from this chapter, partly to avoid endless expansion, and partly because convincing evidence has still to be found for much of it. There are many words and phrases condemned by handbooks and grammars which form part of the speech of nearly all cultivated people, but which are still on precarious footing in literature. These deserve the attention of every interested student of English for a period of several years, to determine their approximate standing and probable future. Some examples from the beginning of the list follow: (words or phrases in italics are the questioned usages) "He treats everyone *alike*"; "They shared the candy *among one another*"; "A doctor is *apt* to be called out at any hour of the night"; "*As long as* the train is late, we may as well return home"; "We've had an *awfully* good time"; and so forth.[1] All these usages are objected to by some textbooks; all of them, it is not unfair to say, are used in good society by cultivated people. This apparent inconsistency must be cleared up by more exact knowledge.

The usages found in the ensuing discussion are all clear-cut matters for which objective evidence is available. While there always has been and probably always will be dispute over the interpretation of the facts concerning a given usage, the facts themselves should prove enlightening.

Above as an adjective. Despite its frequent occurrence in writing (it is less common in speech because it is a writing device) the word *above* as an adjective: "See the *above* statement"; or as a noun: "Refer to the *above*," is the subject of criticism. One textbook says, "*Above*. Undesirable in such use as *the above statement*."[2] The word *undesirable* must imply that objection to the usage is based upon one of the two grounds: either that *above* as an adjective or noun is a neologism, with no standing in literature, or else an older form now obsolescent. It is

---

[1] The entire list will be found at the end of this chapter.
[2] John C. French, p. 344.

not difficult to prove that neither contention can be upheld.

Taking the second first, we find the *New English Dictionary* giving the usage full sanction as follows: "By ellipsis of a pple. as *said, written, mentioned, above* stands attributively, as 'above explanation'; or the noun also may be suppressed and *above* used absolutely as 'the above will show,' etc." To this authority on present usage may be added Hall, who defends it and cites examples.[3] Inasmuch as a long list of examples, both past and present, is attached to the following paragraph, none are offered here as additional support for the currency and acceptability of *above* as an adjective or a noun.

With regard to the use of *above* in literature, Reuben Steinbach offers overwhelming evidence. In spite of its length his list is worth citation as a whole because of its convincing presentation of past and present uses of *above*. He says: [4]

I have seen "the above events" in Thackeray's *Vanity Fair* (Chap. XIV) and "the above ceremony" (Chap. XXII); "the above resolutions" in Dickens' *The Pickwick Papers* (Chap. I); "the above reflections" in George Campbell's *The Philosophy of Rhetoric* (Book I, Chap. I) and "the above passage" (Book I, Chap. II, Section III); "The above specimens will give some idea...." T. L. K. Oliphant's *The Sources of Standard English* (1873), p. 180; "the above tabulations" in John Earle's *English Prose* (1890, p. 39); "the above notes" in W. W. Skeat's *Principles of English Etymology* (Second Series, 1891, p. 258); "the above interjections" in Henry Sweet's *A New English Grammar* (1900, Part I, p. 152); "the above dictionaries" and "the above initial letters" in F. A. March's *Thesaurus Dictionary* (see "Comparative View of Disputed Spellings"); "the above exposition" in Otto Jerpersen's *Chapters on English* (1918, p. 136); "the above

---

[3] J. Lesslie Hall, p. 31.
[4] Steinbach, "On English in Usage," p. 161.

illustration" in Quiller-Couch's *Studies in Literature* (Second Series, 1922, p. 144); "the above list" in Arnold Bennett's *Literary Taste* (Chap. XI); "the above list" in Robert Bridges *On English Homophones* (see *Society for Pure English*, Tract II, p. 18) and "the above motives" in "The Society's Work" (see *Society for Pure English*, Tract XXI, p. 5); "the above words" and "the above list" in H. W. Fowler's *Dictionary of Modern English Usage* (see *hybrid derivations*); "the above propositions" in Bertrand Russell's *Philosophy* (1927, p. 169), and "the above discussion," p. 186; and "the above remarks" in Gilbert Murray's *The Classical Tradition in Poetry* (1927, p. 104).

Included in this list of authors are the names of keen and profound students of the English language who do not scruple to use *above* as an adjective. But it is needless to discuss this matter further. All I wish to say, in conclusion, is that Professor Henderson and the other rhetoricians spoken of attest the weakness of their rule by breaking it themselves.

It is needless to add further discussion. Any writer may feel free at any time to use "The *above* statement," and with only slightly less assurance, "The *above* will prove." In either case he has the authority of scholars and standard literature.

Aggravate for **exasperate.** A textbook writer warns his readers, "Distinguish between aggravate and exasperate." [5] That this distinction is not always observed, not only in colloquial speech but in writing, is fully established by reputable authorities. Professor Krapp says: [6]

Aggravating, adj., strictly should mean *something that makes a bad situation worse, as in His high temperature is an aggravating symptom*. But popularly and colloquially the adjective is used merely in the sense of *annoying or exasperating, as in an aggravating child, Now isn't that aggra-*

[5] Raymond, p. 445.
[6] Krapp, *Comprehensive Guide to Good English*, p. 24.

vating! The past participle *aggravated* is used adjectivally in the same way, as in *I was never so aggravated in my life.*

To Professor Krapp's terms "popularly and colloquially" should be added, "not infrequent in literature." The *New English Dictionary* acknowledges this usage thus: "To exasperate, incense, embitter (a person); *familiar,* to provoke, arouse the evil feelings of." Examples from the literature follow, two of which are here cited: "If both were to aggravate her parents, as my brother and sister do mine . . . ." (Richardson); "Threats only serve to aggravate people in such cases" (Thackeray). Fitzedward Hall also notes that W. D. Howells, in his *Italian Journeys,* used *aggravate* for *provoke.*[7]

Having before them the example, "That boy's mischievous behavior *aggravates* me," the judges of the Leonard-Moffett study[8] placed this usage 79th in a list of 102 items, with a general rating of 3.2 on a scale of 4 points. This rating is low enough to exclude it from the level of cultivated speech or writing, but it is interesting to discover two representative groups of judges who were more liberal. The business men, numbering 24, rated it 2.5, or standard colloquial usage; and 50 teachers of English, members of the English Council, rated it 2.7, or on the outer edge of standard colloquial. The latter score is particularly significant, inasmuch as groups of English teachers are in general very conservative in questions of usage

From all the evidence, then, there seems to be no justification for condemning *aggravate* in the sense of *exasperate* without at least some qualifying statements. This usage is widespread in polite society, it has literary back-

[7] Fitzedward Hall, *Recent Exemplifications of False Philology,* p. 106.

[8] Leonard and Moffett, p. 355.

ing, it is recognized by the *New English Dictionary* and
Professor Krapp, and by two representative groups of
American people. Insofar as the high school is concerned,
objection to it might well be omitted, or subordinated to
a footnote. College textbooks should treat of it more
fully, pointing to it as one of the many examples for the
exercise of taste rather than arbitrary "correctness."

And with the infinitive. Several textbook writers object to the construction employing *and* to join two verbs,
the second of which is usually called an infinitive. One
text says, for example, *"Come to see me, Try to do your
best,* are better English than *Come and see me, Try and
do your best;* though they sound rather stiff and formal
in ordinary convention." [9] These writers make use of the
unfortunate term "better English" as though the construction with *and* were slightly off color, or in bad repute.
As a matter of fact, the construction with *and* is in excellent repute; it has been employed by many careful
writers of the past, and is frequent in the literature and
cultivated spech of today. These examples from the literature show clearly that it has a long history and is not
"inferior English." "At least try and teach the erring
soul" (Milton); "to try and soften his father's anger," "to
try and choose your lot" (Eliot); "How serious a matter
it is to try and resist, I had ample opportunity of experi-
encing" (Matthew Arnold); "To try and teach people
how to live" (Froude).

Contemporary students of language endorse this usage
as standard English. The *New English Dictionary* says,
"And. (10) Connecting two verbs the latter of which
would logically be in the infinitive, especially after go,
come, send, try." Professor Krapp observes, "The con-

[9] Scott and Southworth, Book II, p. 213.

struction is occasionally found in lighter literary style and is well established in cultivated colloquial use." [10] One is tempted to ask whether Professor Krapp would assign the examples cited above to the "lighter literary style" of Milton, Johnson, George Eliot, or Matthew Arnold. Hall lists a number of authorities, and adds, "*Try and* is used several times in Otto Jespersen's books. How can the locution be called a colloquialism with such support in literature?" [11] Professor Curme lists this use as a form of parataxis, saying: [12]

Coördination often indicates a close relation between two words or two propositions, the context frequently showing clearly that one of these is subordinate to the other: ... "You should *try and be reasonable*" (= *to be reasonable*, an abridged infinitive clause in the object relation). "You will *come and see us, won't you?*" (= *to see us*, an abridged adverbial infinitive clause of purpose).

While it may be concluded with full justification that the construction with *and* followed by a verb in parallel construction is standard, fully acceptable English, especially when the verb is *try, go, send, come*, and the like, there is another use of *and* limited to the lighter forms of speech. It appears in such expressions as "Don't *go and* do it now!" "He *went and* hit me," in which the first verb is nothing more than a loose form of intensifier. This construction, although very common in popular speech, must be clearly distinguished from the regular *and* construction in which the intensifier stands in a modifying relationship to the first verb. Notwithstanding the similarity in appearance and syntax, they are quite different in degree of social standing.

[10] Krapp, *Comprehensive Guide to Good English*, p. 40.
[11] J. Lesslie Hall, p. 309.
[12] Curme, *Syntax*, p. 171.

At or in. A rather finely drawn distinction is urged for the preposition used to describe the termination of a journey. "When traveling, we say that we arrive *at* a small town, but *in* a large city." [13] Aside from the fact that strict adherence to such a rule would lead inevitably to the question, "How large must the city be to be entitled to the preposition *in*?" this rule presents a distinction rarely observed by cultivated adults or brought to the attention of beginners in language. Such matters have no place as definite rules in a school text. L. P. Smith says of this usage, "The general rule is that we use *in* for large cities and capitals, *at* for smaller places. There is, however, a notable exception: we commonly use *in* rather than *at* even for a small place if we ourselves are there, probably because then it bulks more largely in our imagination." [14]

Because after reason. The *New English Dictionary* defines the word *because* with the meaning of *that* as "Obsolete. Common in dialects," but it is not clear that the writers had in mind the recently developed construction, "The reason why he spoke was *because* he had to." If they did refer to this use, the term *dialects* will have to include cultivated as well as uncultivated levels, for "the reason was because" is very frequent today in polite conversation, public address, and good writing. Professor Krapp says of this use of *because* "in crude English pleonastically after *reason*," [15] but as the date of publication of his *Guide* is 1927, and the writing probably antedated that by a year or so, no doubt the usage was less common and prominent then than now.

[13] Kimball, Book II, p. 35.
[14] Logan Pearsall Smith, p. 5.
[15] Krapp, *Comprehensive Guide to Good English*, p. 15.

One text says, "Examine the following incorrect sentence: 'His excuse for remaining at home was because he was ill.' The dependent clause is a substantive clause used as subjective complement of the word *excuse*; therefore it should not have the form of an adverbial clause."[16] This advice is traditionally sound, but when an idiom like this establishes itself, earlier grammar must yield. That the idiom is fairly well established in current use is based on the following evidence. The writer has heard it recently in public addresses by Stuart Chase, the noted writer and lecturer, and Professor Curme, the distinguished scholar and linguist, and in others of less note. He has collected these examples from current writing: " . . . the chief reason why it seems so dismal an absurdity is perhaps *because* it could only serve . . . ." (Edith Franklin Wyatt, the *New Republic*); "I suppose that the reason we went to this church . . . was *because* it stood near our home." (Clarence Day, *Harper's Magazine*, December, 1931); " . . . the reason Dickens is so much read in America is *because* he assailed them." (Harris, *Life of Bernard Shaw*, 1931). No diligent search is required to add to these examples; they abound in current writing of the better sort.

There is no need to force this usage upon those who by taste or training find it objectionable. They may continue to avoid it. But there is equally no need to condemn it in the writing of school-children, who are reflecting in its use a natural and common idiom, so far established as to be not eschewed by speakers and writers of respectable attainments.

Between with more than two. There is unanimous agreement in the textbooks that the preposition *between*

16 Clippinger, pp. 445, 446.

may be used only when the object consists of two persons or things; that more than two must be preceded by *among*. The rules are similar to this: " . . . correctness requires that *between* be used when the object represents two persons or things, and that *among* be used when the object represents more than two persons or things."[17] The distinction made by these rules was first insisted upon in the eighteenth century, though even then it was felt to be a formal rather than an actual distinction. "Johnson's *Dictionary* says, '*Between* is properly used of two, and *among* of more; but perhaps this accuracy is not always preserved.' It certainly was not in the title to Trusler's work, *Distinctions between Words Esteemed Synonymous,* for he distinguishes meticulously between all the members of groups of as many as nine words."[18]

In the Leonard-Moffett report the sentence, "A treaty was concluded *between* the four powers" was placed 27th in a list of 102 items, with a rating of 2.3 on a scale of 4 points. This rating indicates that the judges felt it to be cultivated, informal English. It is interesting to note, however, that the teachers of English rated it 2.7, reflecting, no doubt, the influence of the textbooks which are very explicit in this instance.[19]

The *New English Dictionary* is quite positive in its assertion that, "In all senses, *between* has been from its earliest appearance, extended to more than two. It is still the only word available to express the relation of a thing to many surrounding things severally and individually . . . ." There are many examples, one of which is added here, "There were six, who collected between them 15s., 4d." (Cowper).

[17] Kirby and Carpenter, Book VIII, p. 323.
[18] Leonard, *Doctrine of Correctness in English Usage, 1700-1800,* p. 113.
[19] Leonard and Moffett, p. 353.

An interesting example is to be found in Whitney, who in describing the uses of the comparative and superlative degrees, says, "The comparative degree strictly implies a comparison between two objects, the superlative *between more than two*." [20]

It is clear from the evidence that *between* has two legitimate uses in modern English for which the present rules are inadequate. The first use (and the more common one) is that involving two persons or things in which *between* denotes a division into two, or a position in space interior to the designated objects or persons: "Divide the cake *between* Mary and John," "Sit *between* Mary and John," "The bush was planted *between* the two trees." The second use is that in which *between* denotes a distinction in several persons or objects considered individually: "The five diplomats settled the question *between* them," "Distinguish carefully *between* the five uses of the subjunctive"; the underlying psychology is that of distinguishing between any two of a larger number. On the other hand, when a group of more than two is treated as a group, or collectively, the preposition *among* is regularly used: "Divide this *among* the members of your class," "Plant this *among* the shrubs." It is incorrect, therefore, to state arbitrarily that *between* may never be used with more than two.

Can and may. The judges of the Leonard-Moffett study were far more liberal in their acceptance of the word *can* used to denote permission than are the textbook authors. The use of *can* in the sentence, "*Can* I be excused from the class?" was rated 2.3 on a scale of 4 points by the American linguists, and 2.0 by the British linguists. [21]

[20] Whitney, *Essentials of English Grammar*, p. 87.
[21] *Ibid.*, p. 353.

Either rating indicated clearly that in the minds of the judges this use of *can* is "cultivated" informal English and is fully acceptable in the usual language of speech and writing. The school-books, on the other hand, insist firmly that *can* may never be used in asking permission. Curiously enough, the text which devotes most space to the correction of this "error" employs it elsewhere in a model exercise designed to stimulate children's writing. The writer says, " . . . *can* is a greedy and aggressive verb. It gets into every sentence in which it belongs, and it often crowds into sentences in which *may* properly belongs. Therefore, many people use *can* where it should not be used, where it is not correctly used. Remember that *can* does not ask for nor give permission; *can* is correctly concerned only with power or ability. Do you use the words correctly?" [22] But in spite of this warning *can* was permitted to crowd into a sentence, "in which *may* properly belongs" in a composition exercise which begins, "Say, Mary, why *can't* I come to your old party?" [23] From the context it is perfectly clear that the speaker lacks neither "power" nor "ability" to attend the party; it is "permission" which is denied. Yet according to the authors of the book *can* "does not ask or give permission." Then why is *can* used in the opening sentence of a model exercise? Quite clearly because it is customary usage and attracts no attention. Compare it with the "correct" form, "Say, Mary, why *mayn't* I come to your old party?" to discover how odd and unusual the *may* form is. In polite usage, when the auxiliary comes first, as in a question, there is a tendency to distinguish between *may* for permission and *can* for ability. But when an interrogative particle precedes, especially in a negative sentence, *can't*

[22] Kirby and Carpenter, Book VIII, p. 164.
[23] *Ibid.*, p. 232.

is vastly predominant over *mayn't* or *may not,* as in, "Why *can't* I go out tonight?" the distinction may be summed up more clearly by saying that while *may* and *can* in their simpler forms are frequently used discriminatingly, *can't* is largely preferred to express denial of permission or ability.

Some interesting, though perhaps not conclusive, evidence is furnished by a study of telephone conversations. In this study the word *can* was used 396 times and *can't* 228 times, a total of 624 occurrences as compared with 60 uses of *may. Mayn't* was not used at all.[24] It is not unfair to assume that even though the 60 times that *may* was used might include all the situations in which permission was granted, some of the 228 cases of *can't* were to deny permission, inasmuch as *mayn't* was not used at all. In other words, it seems clear that *can't* is employed regularly for *may* and *can* in negative contexts.

Dived or dove. The past tense *dove* of the verb *to dive* is "not in the best use," says one textbook.[25] Inasmuch as *dove* is widespread in popular speech and is by no means unknown in the drawing-room, it remains only to determine whether or not it has a place in literature. Professor Krapp obviously prefers *dived,* but says, *dove* also is in permissible use.[26] The *New English Dictionary* calls it "U. S. and Eng. dialectal form," but quotes Hays, 1867, "The whole herd . . . *dove* down with a tremendous splash." From the returns of the Leonard-Moffett study it appears that the usage is far more acceptable in the United States than in Great Britain, inasmuch as the American judges rated it 2.8 (on the outer edge of ac-

[24] French, Carter, and Koenig, pp. 11, 13.
[25] Scott and Southworth, Book II, p. 252.
[26] Krapp, *Comprehensive Guide to Good English,* p. 202.

ceptability) and the British judges rated it 3.8 (almost illiterate).[27] Yet it occurs twice, not in conversation, in J. B. Priestley's *Good Companions.* J. Lesslie Hall quotes John Earle as saying, "The preterit *dove* of the verb *dive* survives not only in the poetry of Longfellow but also in American prose." [28] Hall, however, is not inclined to accept the full value of this comment, for he adds, "Earle's statement is rather apt to mislead the student. . . . *Dived* is certainly supreme in polite society and in literature, but *dove* has great vitality in 'popular talk.'" [29]

If Hall's summary was true for the time in which he wrote it, we must then conclude that the "vitality in popular talk" of which he speaks is responsible for its now greater frequency. It is no longer true to say that *dived* is supreme in polite society and in literature, for in many sections of the country *dove* is the normal past tense for people of culture, and current writing, especially in the literary periodicals, uses *dove* often enough to challenge the supremacy of *dived.* As a matter of taste *dived* may be preferred, but there is no doubt that *dove* is correct.

We may conclude with Professor Krapp that *dived* has been the "conventionally 'correct' form, but the latter [*dove*], following the analogy of *drive, drove, ride, rode,* etc., is a natural formation, and, in spoken use at least, is perhaps more frequently heard than the former." [30]

Due to. The use of the phrase *due to* to introduce an adverbial modifier is much condemned, especially by writers of handbooks for college composition. Professor Krapp, who is generally inclined toward the liberal side

[27] Leonard and Moffett, p. 354.
[28] J. Lesslie Hall, p. 78.
[29] *Loc. cit.*
[30] Krapp, *Modern English,* p. 292.

in discussions of this sort, says, "Often incorrectly used as a conjunctive adverb (would not the preposition be better?) as in *The battle was lost, due to the lack of ammunition.* The better form would be *The battle was lost, owing to the lack of ammunition,* or *because of,...*" [31] The question arises, why is *owing to* permissible in this construction while *due to* is not? The textbooks also agree in condemning *due to* as follows:

Due to is faulty in such use as: Due to the rain the exercises were postponed. Let it agree with a noun, as in: the postponement was due to rain.[32] *Due to ...* is used to introduce adjective phrases only." [33]

In an article entitled "The Dangling Participle *Due,*" Professor Kenyon discusses at length the history and development of this usage. *Due,* like *owing,* is a participle. Both these words in their earlier use modified substantives. But like other participles they had a tendency to "dangle"; that is, to become detached from a specific substantive and modify instead a phrase or a clause.[34] In this evolution the word *owing* has gone all the way, gaining complete emancipation from participial use in the phrase *owing to,* which is partly prepositional. It may therefore introduce an adverbial modifier with perfect impunity. *Due to,* on the other hand, has lagged somewhat behind in this evolution, and is on that account frowned upon in spite of the parallel development of *owing to.*

This adverbial-prepositional use of *due* is evidently widespread. But its spread appears to have been recent; no dictionary I have seen mentions it. It is my impression that it is

[31] Krapp, *Comprehensive Guide to Good English,* p. 210.
[32] John C. French, p. 345.
[33] Raymond, p. 458.
[34] Cf. discussion of dangling modifiers in Chapter V, pp. 107 ff.

found rarely, if at all, in masters of English style; but those so considered are usually conservative. . . . Its frequency is certainly greater among the less educated, but it appears to be rapidly working its way upward, for some highly respectable writers admit it. It seems to be about equally common in America and England.[35]

Some of his examples are added here: [36]

"The population of Pennsylvania increased from 50,000 in 1730 to more than 200,000 in 1763, *due* in largest part to the thousands of Scotch Irish. . . ." (Charles McLean Andrews); "*Due* to the lack of stress on the last syllable, the *h*-sound disappeared" (E. W. Burlingame); "*Due* largely to the absence from the country of the Committee on Academic Freedom . . . its report has been delayed two years" (*Bulletin of American Association of University Professors*); "Largely *due* to the literary activities of Alfred the Great, . . . the language of Wessex became accepted. . . ." (George H. McKnight); "Immigration . . . from other parts of Brazil has been large, *due* to the rubber excitement" (Colonel George Earl Church); "Suppose, for example, that, *due* to one exigency or another, the lecturer has to become a traveling salesman" (John B. Watson); "America, where women began to predominate from pioneer times, *due* to their scarcity and greater demands" (Count Keyserling); "Whether *due* to her persistence, or to the fact that the official they saw was an old school friend of Jolyon's, they obtained permission for Holly to share the single cabin" (John Galsworthy). And on the brass tablet in front of the Old State House, Philadelphia, is this: "Here the Continental Congress sat from the date it convened . . . except when it sat in Baltimore . . . *due* to the temporary occupation of Philadelphia by the British army."

In recording the foregoing examples of the development and present use of *due to* as a preposition, I should like to make my own position clear. I neither approve nor condemn its use. My speech-feeling is against it; I do not use it, and it always offends my grammatical prejudices. . . . On the other

[35] Kenyon, p. 68.
[36] *Ibid.*, p. 70.

hand I am forced to recognize the facts. *Due to* as a preposition has traveled precisely the same path as the now accepted *owing to.* . . . Undoubtedly it began with the less educated, where it is still most common; but so did hundreds of changes in usage and pronunciation that have attained the best of standing. In fact, there is no surer guarantee of permanence to a new language development that has gained general currency than having a widespread basis in popular practice. Strong as is my own prejudice against the prepositional use of *due to,* I greatly fear it has staked its claim and squatted in our midst alongside of and in exact imitation of *owing to,* its aristocratic neighbor and respected fellow-citizen.

Each other; one another. The grammarians of the school-books insist upon a distinction in meaning between *each other* and *one another,* pointing out that the first must be used for two only, and the second for more than two. Such a distinction does not exist outside of textbooks, for the common use of cultured people as well as the use of standard authors over a long period of time is free from any distinction in meaning. Yet the texts say clearly: "Use *each other* in speaking of two, and use *one another* in speaking of more than two." [37] Professor Krapp also follows tradition rather than usage in this instance, saying, "*each other,* properly used as referring to only two; for more than two the correct form is *one another.*" [38] The *New English Dictionary,* on the other hand, denies any distinction at the outset, saying, "*each other*: used as a reciprocal pronoun in acc., dat., or gen. case; equals *one another.*"

Some examples from various sources show how free from distinction literary usage has been in this matter. "The Church and Christ congratulate one another" (The

[37] Clippinger, p. 236.
[38] Krapp, *Comprehensive Guide to Good English,* p. 212.

Canticles); "These two imparidised in one another's arms" (Milton); "Fowls that live by blood eat not each other" (Trevisa); "These two were great enemies to one another" (Addison); "Sixteen ministers, who met weekly at each others' houses" (Dr. Johnson); "The citizens of different states should know each others' characters" (Webster). Still more interesting is the use of both forms in the same sentence, meaning more than two: "It is a bad thing that men should hate each other; but it is far worse that they should contract the habit of cutting one anothers' throats without hatred" (Macaulay).

Each other with more than two in the sentence, "The members of that family often laugh at each other," was placed 16th in a list of 102 items with a rating of 2.0 by the judges of the Leonard-Moffett inquiry.[39] This rating means that it was considered fully acceptable by more than 75 per cent of the judges; 6 in fact, called it "literary or formal English."

With such convincing evidence from dictionaries, studies of usage, and the literature itself that *each other* may be used interchangeably with *one another*, there is no justification whatever for the textbook rules which try to make a distinction between them.

Either, neither, with more than two. By common custom *either* or *neither* is used when speaking of two, and the phrases *anyone, not one,* or *not anyone* for more than two. According to the textbooks and some authorities the words *either* and *neither* are strictly limited to the use with two, and may not be used correctly of more. So we find, *"Either, neither,* designates one of two persons or things, not one of three or more,"[40] and from Professor

[39] Leonard and Moffett, p. 353.
[40] Raymond, p. 459.

Krapp, "The pronouns *either, neither,* are correctly used only when the choice is between two." [41]

Nevertheless, *either* and *neither* are sometimes used of more than two, and have fair literary authority for such use. The *New English Dictionary* says, "either sometimes = each (of more than two things) (1867, Howells, 'Just above the feet, at *either* of the three corners is an exquisite female bust')." Richard Grant White, the American purist and pedant, used *either* and *neither* in his *Life and Genius of Shakespeare* thus: "That he wrote the plays that bear his name we know; but, except by inference, we do not know the years in which *either* of them was first performed. . . . Peasant, yeoman, artisan, tradesman, and gentleman could then be distinguished from each other (*sic!*) almost as far as they could be seen. Except in cases of unusual audacity, *neither* presumed to wear the dress of his betters." [42]

J. Lesslie Hall records having found *either* and *neither* with more than two in Poe, Emerson, O. W. Holmes, W. D. Whitney, C. Collins, H. W. Mabie, J. F. Genung, and John Earle. "Genung's own rule (*either,* to be used of two objects; *anyone* of more than two) is too strict for him to obey, because it is stricter than the language itself." [43] We may conclude with Hall that *either* and *neither,* although generally employed with two, may occasionally be used with more than two because the rules limiting these words to use with two are stricter than actually observed usage. It is proper to point out, however, that the use with more than two is somewhat rare.

[41] Krapp, *Comprehensive Guide to Good English,* p. 217.
[42] I am indebted to Fitzedward Hall for these illustrations. See also Hodgson, *Errors in the Use of English,* p. 22, for additional examples.
[43] J. Lesslie Hall, p. 86.

Further, farther. Some textbooks set up a distinction between the uses of *farther* and *further* by some such rule as this: "Careful writers use *farther* of actual space, and *further* of degree." [44] While there is no doubt that some writers as a matter of taste have made this distinction, there is also no evidence that the distinction is so universal in literature as to become regimented. Professor Leonard found no reference to it in the eighteenth century other than that in Johnson's *Dictionary*, in which he allowed either use to both words.[45] This is a powerful argument from silence that no distinction was felt in the eighteenth century, a fact further supported by some quotations to follow later. The nineteenth century evidently discovered and fostered the distinction between *farther* and *further*, although some of the best grammars, like Whitney's, failed to mention it.

Professor Curme gives a very clear and sane description of the uses of *farther* and *further* in saying: [46]

We use *farther* and *further* with the same local and temporal meaning, but *further* has also the meanings *additional, more extended, more;* "The cabin stands on the *farther* (or *further*) side of the brook." "I shall be back in three days *at the farthest* (or *at the furthest*)." But: *further* details; without *further* delay. "After a *further* search, I found her." "Have you anything *further* (= *more*) to say?" In adverbial function *farther* and *further* are used indiscriminately: "You may go *farther* (or *further*) and fare worse." There is, however, a decided tendency to employ *further* to express the idea of additional, more extended action: "I shall be glad to discuss the matter *further* with you."

But compare "Do you wish to press the matter *farther*

[44] John C. French, p. 345.
[45] Leonard, *Doctrine of Correctness in English Usage, 1700-1800*, p. 289.
[46] Curme, *Syntax*, pp. 501, 502.

(or *further*)?" in which current usage is about equally divided between the two forms.

Professor Krapp also points out the true distinction, saying that "*farther* [is] the comparative degree of *far*, with a variant *further* in the sense of *more far, more distant*. But in the sense of *in addition, also, more*, . . . the form *further* is the one usually employed." [47] Another writer says, "Some teachers and grammarians make a distinction between the use of *farther* and *further*. . . . Usage does not support this distinction. The two forms seem to be used interchangeably." [48]

All the foregoing discussion may be summed up as follows: *farther* and *further* may be used interchangeably in all meanings but that of *in addition*, or *more*, in which *further* is preferred.

An interesting example of the reversal of the usual rules for *farther* and *further* occurs in Lane's translation of the *Arabian Nights* (London, 1821) which he makes read, "Aladdin's mother pressed him no *farther* but left him at liberty to sit where he pleased." In this sentence *farther* clearly has the meaning of *in addition*, or *more*, a use customarily denied it. Two pages further occurs " . . . as he had a mind to carry him *further* to execute his design...." in which *further* clearly means *more far* in space. There are several similar instances in the same work.

The sanction given to the interchangeable use of *farther* and *further* does not, however, extend to the phrase "all the farther" in the sense of "as far as." While such sentences as, "This is all the farther the train goes," are extremely common in popular speech, especially in the western part of the United States, this locution has no

[47] Krapp, *Comprehensive Guide to Good English*, p. 239.
[48] Cross, p. 290.

standing in cultivated English, either spoken or written. Usage may eventually make it an accepted idiom, but that time has not yet arrived.

Uses of the verb get. Despite the very common use of *have got* or more particularly the construction *'ve got* to signify simple possession in speech and writing, the text-books object to it strongly on the grounds of logic or "correctness." Thus one says, "The verb *get* means 'obtain' and the verb *have* means 'possess.' Do not use these verbs together. When I say 'I have a book,' I mean that I have obtained it [note the extreme confusion of words in this explanation in which *have* is used in two entirely different senses, and *obtain* is hopelessly confused with *get* and *have!*]; therefore it is not only unnecessary but actually wrong to say 'I have got a book.'" [49] The use of the words "actually wrong" is unfortunate, for it is not difficult to prove that the linguistic process by which *have got* comes to mean *have* or *possess* is sound and fully recognized, and furthermore that *have got* has all the support in literature and current usage that can be desired. All the reference materials turned to in defense of *have got* in this section were written prior to the textbook rule above which calls it "actually wrong."

The process by which a perfect tense comes to have present meaning is described tersely by the *New English Dictionary* and more fully by Jespersen. Says the former, "The present tense of *have* forms a present of completed action, or present perfect. Here in origin and form belongs *I have got,* colloquially used for *I have.*" In other words *I have got* originally meant "having obtained (in the past) I now have (in the present)." But as present possession the result of previous getting and present pos-

[49] Pearson and Kirchwey, p. 166.

session detached from the idea of getting are for immediate purposes scarcely distinguishable, it is quite natural that the frequently used *have got* should fade sufficiently to be applied to either situation. Jespersen calls it a pure present. Commenting upon the shifting aspects of tense in certain words, he says: [50]

Some of the old perfects are used exclusively as real presents, e.g. Lat. *Odi, Memini;* in the Gothonic languages the so-called praeteritopraesentia ... e.g. Eng. *can, may,* and Gothic *wait....* To express the perfect-meaning compounds with *have* were then formed: *I have driven, sung, held,* etc. In quite recent times one of these combinations has become a pure present (thus a new perfectopresent verb); *I have got* (*I've got*): the retrospective element is quite absent in *I've got no time....*

So much for scholarly exposition of the process by which *have got* can mean a present *have*. It remains to show that *have got* is used thus in literature and has support in current usage. Hall says: [51]

Besides being recognized by Bradley, Kellner, and Jespersen, *have got* is used by the following writers and speakers of repute: Goldsmith, Lamb, Thomas Hood, Carlyle, Thackeray, A. H. Clough, Gladstone, D. S. Mitchell, Ruskin, Holmes, Sir Henry Taylor, L. Kellner, Dickens. If the names count, *have got* should have some standing and not be branded as a vulgarism. Moreover, it is used too widely in polite society to be so treated.

Moreover, the judges of the Leonard-Moffett study placed *have got* in the sentence, "I *have got* my own opinion on that" number 28 in a list of 102 items, with a rating of 2.3, meaning fully acceptable "cultivated informal English." [52] Inasmuch as these judges included the

[50] Jespersen, *Philosophy of Grammar,* p. 270.
[51] J. Lesslie Hall, p. 122.
[52] Leonard and Moffett, p. 353.

most competent linguists in America and Great Britain, their opinion fully substantiates the claim that *have got* is good current usage. It is evident that the statement, "it is not only unnecessary but actually wrong" is nothing more than uninformed opinion. As such it has no place in a common school textbook.

There is some dispute as to the correct past participle of the verb *get*. Is the form *gotten* obsolescent and out of good current usage, as most of the dictionaries say? May it be tolerated at all? The textbooks call *gotten* "obsolescent," "undesirable," "no longer used"; one text specifically says, "Everyone should notice that the third principal part of *get* is *got* and not *gotten*. The form *got* is preferred by good writers; the older form *gotten* is no longer used by them. It has outlived its usefulness. The correct form is *got*." [53]

So positive a statement as the foregoing excludes *ex cathedra* all writers who use the form *gotten* from the ranks of "good writers." Yet oddly enough, the arch-purist of the nineteenth century, Richard Grant White, although condemning almost everything that came to his attention, vigorously defended *gotten* by saying, "Many persons abbreviate *gotten* into *got*," thus bringing down on his head the wrath of Fitzedward Hall,[54] who opposed *gotten*. But J. Lesslie Hall, after admitting his own earlier objection to *gotten*, cites from his studies a list of fifty authors who used *gotten* ranging from William Caxton to Sir Henry Taylor. In America, though *Webster's Dictionary* of 1864 called it obsolescent, it was used by Poe, Hawthorne, Richard Grant White, W. D. Whitney, Sidney Lanier, and John Burroughs. "In polite society in

---

[53] Kirby and Carpenter, Book VII, p. 176; Book VIII, p. 314.
[54] Fitzedward Hall, *Recent Exemplifications of False Philology*, p. 65.

large parts of America, the longer form has wide vogue in spite of some popular dictionaries." [55] There is every evidence that *gotten* is still alive and flourishing in modern English on both sides of the Atlantic, and that many "good writers" use it naturally and correctly.

The present writer feels a distinction between the uses of *got* and *gotten,* however, which is different from that noted by other writers on the subject. In the uses of the past participle with *have* to imply simple possession or necessity, the form *got* seems to be almost invariably selected. "*I've got* no time"; "*He's got* to go"; "*We've got* the tickets." But in the sense of fetch or obtain, or with certain prepositions, *gotten* seems frequently preferred, as in, "This book was *gotten* from the library"; "having *gotten* us up"; "The point was *gotten* over very clearly." This observation receives considerable support in the fact that for all the uses of *have* with *got* quoted by Hall as meaning possession, *have gotten* does not occur; on the other hand, in the quotation for *gotten* alone, the meaning is always that of "obtain," "secure," or else "move" as in, "His right hand, and his holy arm, hath *gotten* him the victory." (King James Bible); " . . . so soon as we were *gotten* out of hearing"; "The sun had now *gotten* much higher." (Stevenson). If any rule for *got* and *gotten* is necessary, it ought to explain clearly that for sentences in which the meaning of *get* is to obtain, secure, or move, either *got* or *gotten* may be used as past participle; when the meaning is that of possession *got* with some form of *have* is invariably used.

If for whether. May *if* be used to introduce a noun clause implying uncertainty or doubt? Is it correct to say, "I do not know *if* he can come"? Two texts answer defi-

[55] J. Lesslie Hall, pp. 111, 112.

nitely in the negative: "*If* should not be used for *whether.*"
I don't know *whether* (not *if*) I can." [56] And also, "*If.*
Do not use as synonymous with *whether.*" [57] Another text
does not mention the noun clause use of *if,* but insists
that whenever *whether* is used it must be followed by the
phrase *or not* either expressed or implied. If the complementary phrase may be omitted, as is the case when it is
merely implied, one wonders why the issue is raised at
all.

In the eighteenth century Leonard found only one
objection to *if* for *whether,* in the dictionary of J. Johnson, 1763. Here it was listed as a Scotticism in Hume's
Political Discourses. [58]

The history and authority of this usage are ably presented by A. J. F. Zieglschmid, who calls to attention the
linguistic relationship of English *if* to the German *ob,*
cognate words, each originally used to introduce conditional clauses or noun clauses of doubt. In German the *ob*
has become specialized to noun clauses, *wenn* taking its
place in conditional clauses. [59]

In identically the same way, English *if* was originally used
in these same categories. In the course of time, however, the
use of *if* became so intimately associated with conditional
clauses (contrary to the German development) that it became in literary English largely restricted to this category.
For this reason the use of *if* in noun clauses seems inappropriate to our "purists with idiosyncratic notions." The fact,
however, has to be recognized that in spite of these teachings
of these purists *if* is still widely used to introduce noun
clauses, as this old historic usage is deeply rooted in natural
feeling. The modern conjunction *whether* may, of course, be
preferred in literary language.

[56] Raymond, p. 459.
[57] John C. French, p. 345.
[58] Leonard, *Doctrine of Correctness in English Usage, 1700-1800,*
p. 159.
[59] Zieglschmid, p. 50.

Concluding an article in which he shows that many writers of rules violate their own precepts, Reuben Steinbach says: [60]

In ending the discussion of *if* for *whether*, I should like to point out that euphony should at times determine one's choice between the two conjunctions. For example, the sentence, "He was asked if he knew when his friends would speak" reads more smoothly, I think, than it would read if *whether* were used after "asked." On the other hand, the word *if* after "knew" would clearly be less desirable than *whether*.

I have said enough to prove that in a sentence not involving the consideration of euphony, *if* may be used for *whether* to introduce a noun clause following the verbs see, ask, doubt, know, wonder, or the like.

Like as a conjunction. The use *of like* as a conjunction is a usage on the borderline of acceptability in American English. In spite of its comparative infrequency in literature, in spite of the solemn warnings of grammarians and writers of handbooks on usage, and in spite of the active hostility of generations of school-teachers, *like* has firmly established itself in the speech of many sections of the United States, and, if we may judge from current dramatic literature, it is common in many parts of England. In those parts of the United States where it is common, particularly the middle- and far-western portions, college presidents, public lecturers, and leading clergymen—men and women of otherwise impeccable speech—use *like* freely as a conjunction with no sense of sin. The English teachers of these sections either bow to the inevitable and grudgingly admit the usage, or else persist in a never ending and futile attack upon it.

Needless to say, the textbooks are unanimously

[60] Steinbach, "On Usage in English," p. 161.

opposed to admitting the conjunction *like* to accepted usage, saying in effect, "... *like* and *unlike* are incorrectly used as conjunctions. They should be used as prepositions and not as conjunctions." [61] Inasmuch as the authors of these texts are very largely residents of the East Coast, where the usage is less common, or have been trained in Eastern institutions, this unanimity is not surprising. The recognition by textbooks of local variations of acceptability in English usage is reserved for a later day.

Although *like* as an isolated conjunction is not a recent use, having been employed by Shakespeare and his predecessors, it was usually considered an abridgment of *like as* and was not objected to. Professor Leonard records that *like* as a conjunction was "neither used nor mentioned in 18 C. grammars." [62] That it was common in the nineteenth century, however, even creeping into the literature, is witnessed by these examples collected by Hodgson: [63]

"Bidding the customers *like* Queen Eleanor did Fair Rosmund" (Mayhew, 1864); "A timid nervous child *like* Martin was" (*Ibid.*); "And if each man would only add his mite, *like* the pilgrim adds his stone to the heap in the desert...." (Js. Bromfield, 1866); "A nation must laugh ... *like* a satyr, or *like* those bitter fisher women did in France ..., or *like* we have laughed under Punch's auspices for many years." (J. Hain Friswell, 1870); "... the coin is produced *like* wine is produced in bottles...." (Bonamy Price, 1869); "Then, with ingenuous vanity, and forgetting grammar in gush, he (C. Dickens) protests: 'Nobody will miss her *like* I shall.'" (*Temple Bar*, May, 1873).

[61] Kirby and Carpenter, p. 237.
[62] Leonard, *Doctrine of Correctness in English Usage, 1700-1800*, p. 260.
[63] Hodgson, p. 118.

The writer has seen the conjunction *like* in the dialogue of recent plays by Galsworthy, Shaw, Drinkwater, and Philpotts. The attention of some British critics who are pleased to call *like* a "vulgar Americanism" is directed to a study of the dialects of rural England uncontaminated by contact with American vulgarity.

The conjunction *like* is discussed with unusual impartiality in Professor Krapp's *Modern English*. He says: [64]

The use of *like* as a conjunction arises from the ellipsis of a fuller form, *like as*, in the verse in the Psalms, "Like as a father pitieth his children," etc. In the simplification of this double conjunction it happens that the second half is the one which has most generally persisted and the one which the formal grammarian would raise to the position of standard. But the ellipsis of *as*, leaving *like* for the simplified conjunction, is just as natural and just as reasonable, and so we find it in use side by side with *as*. . . . A colloquialism *like* as a conjunction may be, but indefensible it certainly is not. It is first of all a widespread custom of the speech, it has arisen naturally and in the same way that *as* has, and unless one starts from the *a priori* position that there is only one legitimate form of expression for every idea in speech, it makes as strong a bid for favor as the conjunction *as*.

Elsewhere he adds, "For like as a conjunction both the spoken and the written language supply evidence to aid him who should seek to justify this particular form of English speech." [65] The present writer however, has never seen this use in any of the books of Professor Krapp which he has read. Professor Curme, after a brief note on the older English *like as*, says, "The present tendency in colloquial and popular speech is to simplify these forms to *like*: 'It looks *like* he was afraid.'" [66]

---

[64] Krapp, *Modern English*, p. 320.
[65] Krapp, *The Knowledge of English*, p. 180.
[66] Curme, *Syntax*, pp. 282, 283.

Most for almost. "*Most* means a great number, or in a great degree—while *almost* means nearly or not quite. These words cannot be used for each other." [67] Yet despite this warning, which is repeated in several other texts the word *most* frequently occurs in speech and sometimes in writing as a substitute for *almost.* The *New English Dictionary,* although it calls *most* in this use "Obsolete except in dialect," also adds, "It is doubtful whether this is not merely an aphetic form of *almost;* it is often written 'maist, 'most." Krapp also conceives of it as a clipped form as he writes it "most" adding, "dialectal for *almost.*" [68] In the combinations "most all," "most anyone," "most everybody," especially in initial positions, *most* has some standing. That it cannot be freely substituted for *almost* is seen in such examples as, "He *most* won the prize," "John was *most* the only one there," which are unusual to the point of absurdity. But in "*Most* everyone has seen this picture," and "*Most* all of my friends were older than I" the use of *most* may be tolerated if not commended. Leonard sums up this use thus, "'Most all' for 'almost all,' though it has no clear dictionary backing, is nevertheless so common in informal speech among people of at least average culture that it seems a point of pedantry or of rather extreme cultivation to object to it." [69] While *most* for *almost* cannot be defended in formal literary style, there is no reason for condemning it in elementary school-books. It is at least common enough to be permitted in speech and in the informal writing of children.

Myself for I, or me. A correspondent voices his objection to *myself* in *American Speech* thus: "A layman...

[67] Kimball, Book I, p. 46.
[68] Krapp, *Comprehensive Guide to Good English,* p. 398.
[69] Leonard, "Usage Notes," p. 252.

is particularly distressed to see you permit the ridiculous practice that is in such very common use of substituting 'myself' for 'me' in such a sentence as the one you give, 'They invited my friends and myself'; no one would say, 'They invited myself.'" [70]

There are two points of particular interest in this extract; one is the admission of the great currency of the usage, and the other is the confusing of the use of *myself* as sole object of a verb with the use of *myself* as the second member of a compound object. As a matter of fact there are five distinct uses of *myself* as the substitute for a personal pronoun, disregarding the reflexive uses, ranging in acceptability from obsolescence to current standard usage. They are:

1. *Sole subject of a verb.* EXAMPLE: *"Myself* when young did eagerly frequent doctor and saint...." (Fitzgerald). Archaic, poetic, not acceptable in current prose usage, though good English in poetry.

2. *Second member of a compound subject.* EXAMPLE: "John and *myself* brought the Yule log home." Frequently heard, but not fully enough established to gain recognition. Nevertheless it was frequently used in this manner by Washington in his personal correspondence, in sentences like the following: "From the moment Mrs. Washington and *myself* adopted the two youngest children...."

3. *After comparisons with* than. EXAMPLES: "Enough to make a better man than *myself* ... run into madness." (Richardson). Acceptable, informal usage, not at all rare in literature. Similarly after as: "No one knew this as well as *myself.*"

4. *Sole object of a verb or preposition.* EXAMPLE: "To *myself,* mountains are the beginning and the end of all natural scenery." (Ruskin). Not quite as acceptable in current usage as number 5. (This use must of course

[70] *American Speech,* Vol. IV, p. 252.

not be confused with the simple reflexive as in "I read to *myself*.")

5. The second or later member of a compound object of a verb or preposition. EXAMPLE: "He . . . invited John Wilson and *myself* to visit him for a day or two." (Lockhart, *Life of Sir Walter Scott*). This use is fully established in literature and current English.

The textbooks make no effort to distinguish these various uses of *myself*, condemning it altogether as a substitute for the personal pronoun. Two examples will serve to show their point of view:

1. "In speaking of yourself with others never use the pronoun *myself*." [71] Note that this rule prohibits such a sentence as "I gave a folder to all present, not omitting *myself*," a sentence fully acceptable in literary usage.

2. "There is one misuse against which you should be warned. It is seen in the following sentences: Father, mother, and *myself* were all going. The teacher gave problems to John, Mary, and *myself*." [72] In this rule there is no attempt to distinguish between the nominative and objective uses of *myself*, although in actual usage there is much greater authority for the latter than for the former. The rules in the other texts are similar.

The two uses of *myself* as a substitute for the personal pronoun which can be defended on the grounds of literary example and current frequency are (1) in the nominative case in a comparison after *than* or *as*; (2) as the second or later member of a compound object. Of the former the *New English Dictionary* says, ". . . *myself* in this use now expresses no special emphasis, being preferred to avoid the awkwardness of *I*." In other words, it is fully acceptable English. Of the second usage it says, "In an enumeration, when not occupying the first

[71] Pearson and Kirchwey, p. 191.
[72] Kirby and Carpenter, Book VIII, p. 272.

place, it does not now express any special emphasis, being in this position commonly preferred to *me*." Examples are given from Layamon to Ruskin. This too is acceptable English.

A further note on the use of *myself* as the second object of an enumeration is found in the Leonard-Moffett study. The average of all the judges for this usage in the sentence, "They invited my friends and *myself*" was 2.4 on a scale of 4 points; the British judges alone gave it 2.0, revealing the fact that the usage is more firmly established in Great Britain than in the United States. Nevertheless the general rating of 2.4 means that the American judges felt it to be well within the range of currently acceptable English.[73]

In a letter to the present writer, the distinguished British linguist and lexicographer Sir William Craigie once wrote, *apropos* of a visit, "I understand you will meet Lady Craigie and *myself* at the station."

There is little doubt that this usage springs either from the desire to avoid making a choice between *I* and *me*, or from the psychological urge to avoid the bluntness of the first person pronoun. *I* and *me* in enumerations or comparisons are direct, forceful, and subjective; *myself* in the same constructions permits an impersonal feeling, an objectifying of the self into the group. It softens the intrusion of the ego; it is felt to be modest, polite, and courteous. From all angles—literary authority, current usage, and psychological need—*myself* as the objective in an enumeration, or as the nominative after *than* or *as* is good English.

Proven. The past participle *proven* is objectionable to many writers of textbooks, who are perhaps influenced in

[73] Leonard and Moffett, p. 355.

this decision by the common dictionaries which call
proven "archaic" or "Scottish." One writer says, "Always
use *proved*. There is excellent linguistic reason for objecting to *proven*," [74] but he fails to show what the
"excellent linguistic reason" is. The principal linguistic
reason for using or avoiding an expression is its standing
in literature and current speech, but one can be sure
that the author quoted above does not have this in mind.
He refers, no doubt, to the assumption that since *prove*
came into English from Latin *probare* through the Old
French *prover* it has no right to an Anglo-Saxon -*n* past
participle as though it were a native strong verb. There
are two good answers to such an objection: first, that
native suffixes are frequently attached to foreign roots
to form a useful word, as in the once much disputed
talented; second, that if *proven* has an honorable history
in English and some standing in current literature and
speech, a doubtful etymology cannot be urged against it.

The *New English Dictionary* recognizes *proven,* saying, "The past participle *proven,* originally Scotch from
prove, follows the strong verbs; e.g. cleave, cloven;
weave, woven," and quotes several authors. Professor
Lounsbury is a strong supporter of it, concluding, "Some
authors of repute employ it; others avoid it.... It is more
than likely that it is destined to establish itself perman-
ently in the language of literature." [75] Hall records having
seen it at least seven times in Tennyson's *Idylls of the
King* and twice in his *Aylmer's Field* ... once in Huxley;
twice in Kipling's serious verse; once in Fitz-Greene
Halleck's poetry; once in Miss Katherine Lee Bate's
Religious Drama." [76] He adds further, "If one great

[74] John C. French, p. 346.
[75] Lounsbury, *Standard of Usage in English,* pp. 62-65.
[76] J. Lesslie Hall, pp. 227-228.

author can establish a form, Tennyson has established *proven*.... In America, *proven* has considerable vogue in polite society and in the best journals." [77]

The present writer has noted two instances in a journal of high literary standing, *Harper's Magazine*. In the issue for August, 1931, appeared an advertisement for books published "By the House of Harper" which began, "*Proven*—Books whose various excellencies have raised them to honors...." In the issue for October, 1931, in an article by Max Eastman entitled, "Poets Talking to Themselves" appears the sentence, "... if only for having so specifically *disproven* the hard saying of Pascal."

It appears from the evidence that *proven* is accredited and acceptable. With long enough standing to be absolved from the charge of being a neologism, it has been used freely by reputable authors of the last half century, it is found regularly in current writing of literary merit, and it is extremely common in speech. No further facts are needed to describe it as standard English.

Real and sure as adverbs. "The worse offenders" says a recent textbook,[78] "are *sure* and *real*. They are used incorrectly to modify verbs, adjectives, and adverbs instead of the adverbs *really* and *surely*." It is scarcely just to lump *real* and *sure* together in this way, for even as adverbs they vary greatly in use and acceptability. There is, for example, an appreciable difference in social level between "This pie is *sure* good," and "This pie is *real* good." Moreover *sure* is frequently used in popular speech as a verb modifier: "We *sure* had a good time," whereas *real* is never used this way. To do them full

[77] *Ibid.*, p. 228.
[78] Kirby and Carpenter, Book VIII, p. 200.

justice, even in condemnation, they must be treated separately.

Sure was once a "flat" adverb, and was commonly used as in this example: "He is *sure* a prince of a royal courage." (George Cavendish, d. 1562, *Life of Thomas Wolsey*). But today, while it is exceedingly common in popular speech, it is almost entirely excluded from polite conversation and careful writing. In fact, the avoidance of *sure* is one of the indications of cultivation in speech; its use is felt to be socially undesirable.

The position of *real* as the modifier of an adjective or adverb is considerably higher. While it cannot be called a formal, polished use it is nevertheless frequently heard in professional and social groups in such sentences as: "It was *real* good of you to come"; "Shall we have a *real* fine day tomorrow?"; "I want everyone to be *real* quiet for a moment." That these uses are natural and proper in informal cultivated speech can scarcely be denied.

In a sentence similar to the last above, "I will write *real* soon," a textbook author substitutes "really soon." [79] This is utter nonsense. No one ever says, "I will write *really* soon." We may say "I will write soon; I will really write soon; I will write soon, really," but never "I will write *really* soon." It simply isn't English. The more one examines the original sentence, the more one becomes convinced that "I will write *real* soon," is by far the most natural and expedite manner of expressing the idea.

Real as the modifier of another adverb in "real quick," "real soon," "real fast," and the like seems to be on the outer edge of acceptability. As the modifier of an adjective, as in "real good," "real bad," "real strong," it is slightly less secure. Nevertheless, the child who is instructed to purchase a bottle of "Carter's *Real* Black

[79] John C. French, p. 290.

Fountain Pen Ink" [80] can scarcely be censured the next day for writing "a *real* dark night" or even "a *real* good boy." He has the example before him on his desk. So does his teacher. It is quite conceivable that forty million ink bottles may establish *real* as the modifier of an adjective. It would be far less remarkable than the establishment of the verb *to kodak* from the name of a commercial product.

Sit and set; lie and lay. The confusion of the parts of the verb *sit* and *set, lie* and *lay* is so widespread in English and is characteristic of speech levels so far above those in which other verb-form errors are common that it may be considered a distinct problem. Many cultivated people otherwise accurate in verb usage admit of considerable uncertainty in the use of these verbs. Discrimination is further confused by certain idiomatic exceptions which will be noted later. The textbooks on the whole are rather clear in their presentation of the transitive and intransitive functions of these verbs; one only of the books examined for this study asserts arbitrarily, "*Lay* is transitive; *lie* is intransitive; *set* is a transitive verb; *sit* is intransitive." [81] The authors may claim with some justice that these rules are for classroom purposes and that to add exceptions and vagaries of usage to the otherwise clear-cut distinction would result in a "confusion worse confounded." Yet so common and correct an idiom as "the sun sets" is ignored or tacitly condemned by the rules as they stand. The matter is admittedly difficult, as Greenough and Kittredge agree: [82]

[80] I think no one will insist that the manufacturers are speaking of Real Black-Ink, in which the adjective modifies a hyphenated noun.

[81] Lewis and Hosic, p. 105.

[82] Greenough and Kittredge, p. 281.

. . . it is not surprising that the distinction between *sit* and *set*, *lie* and *lay* has broken down in vulgar English, and has not always maintained itself in literature. In the first half of the last century *lay* was pretty common for *lie* even in respectable authors. (See examples below.) The sun still *sets*, and it is excessively difficult (hardly desirable) for a poultry farmer to speak of "a *sitting* hen."

It will be interesting to note some of the literary confusion and anomalous idioms. The most common by far is the substitution of *laid* for *lay* (the past tense of *lie*). It is not only heard daily in the speech of cultivated people, but has appeared frequently enough in literature to merit observation. For example: "The Waterloo man was represented by a little child of three; a Martin of course, who *laid* in the gutter." (Kingsley); "The look of immovable endurance which *underlaid* her expression." (Wilkie Collins); "I have *laid* awake upon it." (Trollope); ". . . . I never took off my clothes, but *laid* down in them wrapped in my cloak." (C. J. Matthews); "He again *laid* down and addressed himself to sleep." (De Quincey). Less frequently the confusion of *lie* and *lay* in the present tense occurs in literature. One recalls Byron's "There let him lay"; G. W. Dasent is quoted by W. B. Hodgson as saying, "Dapple had to *lay* down on all fours before the lad could bestride him." [83] The use of *lay* intransitively in the idiom *to lay in wait* is recognized by the *New English Dictionary* thus: "*lay*, intransitive. To lay for; to set an ambush or a trap for; to lie in wait." In nautical terminology occurs also the idiom "to lay out along" as in "The sailors *laid* out along the yards."

Set as an intransitive verb has already been noted in connection with the "setting sun" and the "setting hen." No textbook questions the correctness of "the sun sets,"

[85] Hodgson, p. 37.

but one at least makes an issue of the poultry idiom: "Supply the right form of *sit* or *set*" in the sentences, "The dove is .... on the eggs," "Hens .... on eggs." [84] The child is of course bullied into writing, "The dove is *sitting* on the eggs," and "Hens *sit* on eggs," although he is fully conscious of the real distinction between *sitting* (casually assuming a sitting position) and *setting* (purposefully incubating eggs). If one concedes that the purpose of language is to convey complete and accurate meaning, the idiom "the hen *sets*" is vastly preferable to "the hen *sits*."

The verb *sit* is predominantly intransitive, but it has one or two transitive functions worthy of note. For example, there is a subtle distinction between "set the baby down" and "sit him up." The more formal "set him up" is too general; it denotes any change from a recumbent position. But "sit him up" means specifically "cause him to sit." Similarly "set him here by me" lacks the exactness of "sit him here by me." It is unfortunate that these distinctions, commonplaces of everyday speech, should be tacitly or openly condemned by school-book rules. They should be recognized and commended as types of accuracy far superior to the merely formal accuracy of textbook definitions of "transitive" and "intransitive" verbs.

The foregoing discussion is not a defense of an indiscriminate confusion of the forms *sit* and *set, lie* and *lay.* These words in their normal uses convey clear, distinct, and accurate meanings which are regrettably obscured in much present-day speech. The point the writer wishes to stress is that whenever any of these words ordinarily transitive or intransitive, acquires a new, distinct, and accurate meaning by a shift in function from transitive

[84] Scott and Southworth, Book I, p. 158.

to intransitive, or the reverse, the new use should be defined and accredited instead of being condemned as a violation of purely formal rules. To acknowledge it so is to show a commendable appreciation of the real purpose of language.

Than as a quasi-preposition. The textbooks are firm in their insistence that *than* is always a conjunction and must be followed by a clause or an ellipsis of a clause. In particular they stress the fact that *than* may never be used with *different*. One says, ". . . *than* and *as* are conjunctions and not prepositions." [85] With more specific reference another adds, "Never use the word *than* after the word *different*." [86] This latter rule overleaps itself inasmuch as there is a perfectly good use of *than* after *different* in which *than* is a conjunction. For example: "Is he *different from* his brother?" "He is much more *different than* you would suppose." Attention is called to this construction merely to point out once again the danger of ill-considered rules.

The real question at hand is whether or not *than* may be used after *different* as a quasi-preposition, similar in use to the more common *from*. Curme has no use for this construction, dismissing it with brief comment: "Since *different* has the same meaning as *other*, many improperly employ *than* after it instead of the preposition *from*: 'Your idea is different *than* (instead of the correct *from*) mine.'" [87] But Krapp presents a wider range of evidence: [88]

The construction *different than* though reprehended by the authorities and avoided by careful writers, may nevertheless

[85] Raymond, p. 193.
[86] Kimball, p. 177.
[87] Curme, *Syntax*, p. 303.
[88] Krapp, *Comprehensive Guide to Good English*, p. 195.

be found occasionally in writings of good standing. It is a convenient construction. . . .

Modern purist opinion is very firm against the use of *different than*, but as experienced a writer as H. G. Wells uses it freely. He writes, for example, in one of his prefaces, that a character of his "sees things from a different angle than did Mr. Polly," and a little later occurs the sentence, "They will have a different sort of strategy than the disorganization of political parties and subtler methods than sabotage schemes in cellars and the misdirection of honest discontent." [89]

It must be added, in fairness to Professor Krapp, that he feels that the usage of one or two writers, even those as prominent as H. G. Wells, does not establish a form in English. But we are not dependent upon the usage of a few contemporaries. *Different than* is an old construction, occurring in the works of the best-known English writers. Fitzedward Hall notes this sentence in DeQuincey, "And, apart from that objection, at this period, the hasty unfolding of far *different* intellectual interests *than* such as belong to mere literature. . . ." [90] Elsewhere he notes more fully, "We find as the result of mere heedlessness, *different than* in Addison, Steele, Defoe, Richardson, Coleman and Thornton, Miss Burney, Coleridge, Mr. DeQuincey, Mr. Thackeray, and Dr. Newman." [91] Surely a most respectable list of "heedless" writers. Further examples are offered by Hodgson: ". . . our English poet . . . has given us a picture of a very *different* kind *than* what Homer intended." (Fitzosborne, *Letters*); "The seventeenth century evidently had a *different* notion of books and women *than* that which flourishes in the nineteenth." (*Pall Mall Gazette*, August, 1867);

[89] Krapp, *The Knowledge of English*, p. 208.
[90] Fitzedward Hall, *Recent Exemplifications of False Philology*, p. 21, footnote.
[91] Fitzedward Hall, *Modern English*, p. 82.

"Provision is made for happiness of a quite *different* nature *than* can be said to be made for misery." (W. Smith, *Gravenhurst*.)[92] To which may be added another contemporary use: "See that you use no word in a *different* meaning *than* it was used one hundred years ago." (Walter Hines Page, *Letters*.)

It may be seen, then, that *different than* is no stranger in literature, past or present, and that it is by no means as reprehensible as the textbook writers would have it. While there is little doubt that *different from* is the currently preferred form, *different than* is a possible substitute to be found in reputable writers and polite conversation. In such a sentence as, "My book is different from yours," *than* is undoubtedly avoided by all but the less literate. But in sentences requiring "from that which" to complete the comparison, *than* is a convenient short-cut often employed, as in the sentence of Walter Hines Page above. Current British usage favors the construction *different to;* for example, "This material is *different to* what I expected."

The case of the pronoun after *than* in comparisons is usually nominative, although the accusative appears in popular speech and older literature. On the whole, however, contemporary cultivated speech and writing is quite consistent in the use of the nominative in all constructions but one: the relative pronoun *whom*. Although it is grammatically anomalous, usage has established beyond doubt the objective case of the relative pronoun after *than*. Professor Setzler says: [93]

Than is regularly and properly a conjunction, but after *than* the relative pronoun frequently takes the objective form. The reason for this is not easily explained, but the practice is of

[92] Hodgson, p. 114.
[93] Setzler, *Advanced English Syntax*, p. 79.

long standing in English; it dates at least from the oft-quoted line of Milton, "Satan than *whom* none higher sat." The use of this form for the nominative relative after *than* occurs not only colloquially, but it is also very frequent in the literary language.

Hall cites several examples antedating Milton to show that he did not originate this construction.[94]

Jeremy Taylor says, "and all this for man, *than whom* nothing could be more miserable. . . ." (Date, 1650-51). Richard Hooker says, "Many men there are, *than whom* nothing is more commendable than when they are singled." (Date, *ante* 1600). Sidney says, "so grave counsellors, as besides many . . . *than whom*, (I think) that Realm never brought forth a more accomplished judgment, more firmly builded upon vertue." (About 1581). These passages alone prove that Milton did not originate this phrase, though the fact that he used it in *Paradise Lost* helped no little in giving it wide currency.

Fitzedward Hall takes Cobbett to account for his condemnation of this construction.[95]

Not unlike Mr. White's position regarding ill is that of Cobbett regarding than whom:

"Cromwell, *than whom* no man was better skilled in artifice." A hundred such phrases might be collected from ·Hume, Blackstone, and even from Doctors Blair and Johnson. Yet they are bad grammar. In all such cases *who* should be made use of; for it is nominative and not objective. . . . and, therefore, we should write: "Cromwell, *than who* no man was better skilled in artifice." That anyone but Cobbett would abide this, as English, is highly improbable; and how the expression, a quite classical one, which he discards can be justified grammatically, except by calling its *than* a preposition, others may resolve at their leisure and pleasure.

Enough has been written to show that *than whom* is an ancient and respectable form, fully established in

[94] J. Lesslie Hall, p. 295.
[95] Fitzedward Hall, *Recent Exemplifications of False Philology*, p. 84.

English, though not without occasional protest. Moreover, it persists untouched by the more rigid custom of
modern English demanding the nominative after *than*
which has practically driven out *than him, than her,* and
than them from literary and cultivated usage.

Whose as a neuter possessive pronoun. Modern English
sadly lacks a neuter possessive pronoun, to supply which
lack the masculine-feminine *whose* has been extended
to cover the meaning which must otherwise be expressed
by *of which.* Inasmuch as the latter phrase frequently
necessitates an awkward revision of the sentence in
which it occurs, sometimes obscuring rather than clarify-
ing the meaning, the extension of *whose* is highly commendable as a practical and sensible way out of the
difficulty. But eighteenth-century guardians of the
language, influenced by the restriction of *who* and *whom*
to persons, raised serious doubts about the propriety of
whose in the neuter use, and formulated objections which
later become crystallized into rules. Thus Dr. Johnson
says, "*Whose* is rather the poetical than the regular genitive of *which*"; Bishop Lowth adds, "*Whose,* is, by some
authors, made the possessive case of which...I think
improperly." [96] Priestly comments, "I do not think that
the construction is generally pleasing." Hornsey is more
explicit: "*Which* properly speaking is indeclinable." [97]
These strictures became in time rules which have been
copied from book to book so that today we find statements like this in the current textbooks: "*Whose* is sometimes used also for the possessive of *which,* but the form
of which is better." [98] *Of which* is better only if it is

[96] Fitzedward Hall, *Recent Exemplifications of False Philology,*
p. 6.
[97] Leonard, "Usage Notes," p. 66.
[98] Kimball, p. 126.

either the superior manner of expressing clearly the idea of neuter possession, or if it has decided preference in the literature or current usage of English. The first reason cannot be upheld; *of which* is frequently awkward and devious where *whose* is clear and direct. In answer to the second reason there is so much evidence available that only the limits of space preclude an overwhelming array. F. Hall sums up a long discussion with "...the use *of whose* for *of which* where the antecedent is not only irrational but inanimate, has had the support of high authorities for several hundred years." [99] To this he appends a long list of references. J. Lesslie Hall presents a list of 1,050 passages from 140 authors from Thomas Malory to W. W. Skeat, covering a period of 400 years. He asks: [100]

Are there any authors left to name? The results of this study of the neuter *whose* amaze the present writer; he is fully prepared to endorse the statement made by Lounsbury that this *whose* is used by every author entitled to be called an authority.

In sharp contrast with the textbook grammarians quoted above as saying "*of which* is better English," is the statement of Curme: [101]

In poetry and choice prose the old form is still the favorite: "a little white building whose small windows were overgrown with creepers" (Galsworthy). The use of *whose* for persons and things is the survival of older usage which knew nothing of the differentiation (of *whose* and *of which*).

Professor Krapp also says, "...*whose* has always been freely used as the possessive of neuters." [102]

[99] Fitzedward Hall, *Recent Exemplifications of False Philology*, p. 7.
[100] J. Lesslie Hall, p. 325.
[101] Curme, *Syntax*, pp. 229, 230.
[102] Krapp, *Comprehensive Guide to Good English*, p. 623.

There is no support whatever to the claim that *of which* "is better" than *whose*. The history of the language, the usage of reputable authors, both past and present, and the opinions of qualified linguists all point conclusively to the fact that *whose* is correct, acceptable, and in many instances "better" English.

ITEMS FOR FURTHER STUDY

The words and phrases which are placed below have all been objected to as forms of "incorrect" English. Judged by the standards for the formal, literary essay, many of them are undesirable for such writing, but as has been pointed out in Chapter III, the formal, literary standard is not the only criterion of "correctness." Indeed, many of these uses are established beyond doubt in the informal speech of cultivated people; many others are frequently heard, if not fully approved; and none are definitely illiterate. The attempt to eliminate them from the speech or informal writing of students, even of those in college courses, is as futile as it is wrong. The commendable attitude to take with regard to these less established usages is one of interested inquiry, to determine to what extent they are used, by what people, on what occasions. Only by a number of such observations carefully kept by interested students in various parts of the English-speaking world can anyone arrive at a proper estimate of the standing of the expressions.

The criticized word is underlined in each sentence; the form preferred by the critics follows in parentheses:

1. He treats everyone alike. (similarly)
2. They could not agree among one another. (each other)
3. I very much appreciate the favor you have done me. (?)
4. A doctor is apt to be called out at any hour of the night. (likely)

5. As long as you've bought it, you may as well use it. (Since, As)
6. He caught an awful cold. (bad, severe)
7. A shed was in back of the house. (behind)
8. I read fifteen pages, but I was unable to read the balance of the assignment. (remainder)
9. Don't blame that on me! (blame me for that)
10. Directly I entered I saw something was wrong. (As soon as)
11. Sir Bevidere fulfilled the dying wish of the king. (wish of the dying king)
12. Why does she enthuse over such queer flowers? (become enthusiastic)
13. When do you expect they'll come? (think, predict)
14. Please fix this broken toy. (repair)
15. The ditch was three foot wide. (feet)
16. I guess you'll like it. (think, fancy)
17. You can't help but see. (help seeing)
18. I stayed home all afternoon. (at home)
19. They hung the wretch at five o'clock. (hanged)
20. I love apple pie. (like)
21. Why don't you be nice to her? (kind)
22. He looked out the window. (out of)
23. The work had to be done over again. (over, or again)
24. He will remain providing he is needed. (provided)
25. Next month I am going to have a raise in salary. (rise)
26. The woman had sewn all day. (sewed)
27. We stopped at the hotel three days. (stayed)
28. If he went that far, he must have reached the summit. (so)
29. There are two kinds of drawings which have to be made. (two kinds of drawings have to be made).
30. The man drank three strong cups of coffee. (cups of strong coffee).

31. I was very pleased to meet him. (very much pleased)
32. The old cat came with us a little ways. (way)

This list is not exhaustive, but it does illustrate the kind of usages condemned on general principles, or on personal aversion, by textbook writers. Each of the expressions is worthy of careful study, to determine its history, its place in literature, and its standing in current usage.

PART III

PROCEDURES IN TEACHING USAGE

IX

Foundations in the Elementary Grades

THE PROBLEM

The successful use of good English in adult life rests on a foundation of good habits so thoroughly established as to be automatic. For all ordinary purposes of communication the proficient adult is generally unconscious of language choices; appropriate words, idioms, and constructions flow along unimpeded by conscious effort. Only in unusually formal or difficult situations does he become conscious of the need for closer discrimination in his language choices. Even then, good habits, augmented by experiences gained in observation of the speech and writing of others, carry him through. The laying of sound habits is therefore the first step in teaching good usage.

Language habits established in early childhood lay an almost ineradicable pattern of speech for the remainder of life; consequently the teaching of language use in the early years of childhood is of paramount importance. Young children learn speech by ear; what they hear is what they say. Fortunate indeed is the child who hears from the cradle onward the patterns of English usage which lie within the range of nationally acceptable usage. For him there is no usage problem other than the mastery of new and more mature forms.

Doubly unfortunate is the child who develops within the influence of sub-standard English. He not only forms bad habits of speech in the most impressionable years of his childhood, but he also reinforces these bad habits by countless repetitions prior to the influence of school.

Since a large number of children enter school with undesirable speech habits formed in the home environment, the chief task of language instruction in the early grades is to substitute more desirable habits. This is easy to say but excessively difficult to accomplish. Habits ingrained by years of repetition have an almost invincible persistency; moreover, for most children the undesirable habits are constantly reinforced by continued repetitions in the home. What can the teacher of elementary grades do to correct faulty language habits and lay a foundation of sound habits? From what is known of habit-forming in education, two fundamental principles emerge to govern the teaching of usage in the early school years. It is the purpose of this chapter to state and develop these principles:

1. To break bad habits and to substitute more desirable habits necessitates a very strict limitation on the number of specific items to be attacked in the elementary grades.

2. The items selected for mastery must be taught soundly and thoroughly in accordance with all that is known of the psychology of habit formation.

USAGE ITEMS FOR THE ELEMENTARY GRADES

The principle has been stated that there must be a strict limit to the number of items to be attacked in the elementary grades. Two observations of great significance support this principle:

1. The constant repetition of a relatively small number of errors constitutes over 90 per cent of the usage problem in the elementary grades.[1]

2. A large number of "errors" listed in textbooks and language work books are not errors at all, but are colloquial English appropriate to the speech and writing of young children.

Even if the teacher in the elementary grades limits herself to the correction of those errors that the pupils of her own class make, except in unusually fortunate circumstances she will find many more than she can deal with successfully. Expressions not frequently used and those involving fine distinctions are quite properly postponed at least until the junior or senior high school. It is much better to concentrate on a few forms at a time until the errors are eliminated than to attack too many at once. Moreover, the effort of habit-change is considerable for young children. Their interest and active attention can be secured for only a few specific items of change at any one time.

The following list of errors is presented as a sort of inventory of essential items to attack in the elementary grades, particularly in the first six grades. The wise teacher will not attempt to teach all the items of this list for any one grade, but will select for concentrated attention those of the greatest social penalty and greatest utility at her own grade level. For convenience the items are arranged alphabetically.

[1] Evidence for this observation may be found in the studies of Stormzand and O'Shea, O'Rourke, and many others. See Bibliography, pages 257-261.

A. Errors to Be Attacked for Elimination in the Elementary School

ain't, or *hain't*
hair *are*
a orange
have *ate*
he *begun*
was *broke*
he *brung*
climb (short i)
clumb
he *come*
have *did*
he, she, it *don't*
I *drunk*
didn't, hadn't
ought
was *froze*

he *give*
I *got* for *I've got*
my brother, *he* (and
other double sub-
jects)
her, him and *me*
went
hisself
there *is, was* four
knowed; growed, etc.
learn me a song
leave me go
me and Mary went
haven't *no,* **haven't**
nothing

he *run*
have *saw*
I *says*
he *seen*
them books
theirselves
this here
that there
us boys went
we, you, they *was*
with *we* girls
have *went*
have *wrote*
it is *yourn, hern,*
ourn, theirn

The experienced teacher will recognize in this list the errors typical of the speech and writing of grade-school children, but she will find missing from the list many other errors listed in textbooks, work books, and tests. Consistent with the principle of a restricted number of items to attack, the forms not shown in list A should be ignored so far as class instruction and drill emphasis are concerned. This does not mean that a child who inquires about a particular item should not be given all the information available to the teacher. It does mean that instruction and drill for mastery by the entire class should be limited to a selection of items from list *A*.

As a guide to the individual teacher, and as a basis of agreement among teachers of the various levels of a school system, list *B* is presented to point out certain language forms which may be omitted from class instruction in the first six grades. Leaving them out of class instruction does not mean that they are all to be considered universally acceptable English or that individual pupils of superior ability may not be guided individually to make substitutions for some of these forms. The reason for their omission is that most of them are acceptable in colloquial English.

B. FORMS TO RECEIVE NO CLASS INSTRUCTION IN THE ELEMENTARY SCHOOL

None of us *are, were* there.

Can I go?

Do the work *good*.

I haven't *got* a pencil.

I couldn't *hardly* do the work. I haven't *hardly* any.

She gave it to John and *I*.

He *lays* down every day, is *laying* down, *laid* down, has *laid* down, etc.

Do it *like* I do.

He acts *like* he is cold.

It is *me, him, her, them*.

Everybody, everyone said that *they*. . . .

Who did you choose?

If I *was* you, I'd play ball. I wish I *was* you.

Who are you waiting for?

I *will* probably be late.

One of my brothers *were* here.

EFFECTIVE TEACHING PROCEDURES

Of equal importance with the selection of a limited number of items to teach is the employment of sound teaching practices. Before discussing these, however, it will be well to consider some of the popular fallacies connected with the teaching of correct usage.

Reliance on grammar. This fallacy arises from the assumption that an error in a verb form (he done it) is corrected by teaching the pupil the principal parts of the verb *to do;* or that a pronoun error (him and me went home) is corrected by teaching the declension of the pronoun. The approach to correctness through grammar may have some validity for the adult who has developed the power to reason and arrive at conclusions from particular instances. For the young child, however, the evidence [2] is definitely negative. Childen's speech is the product of habits, as has been pointed out. Any change effected in the speech of children will come about by providing new habits and an environment in which the new habits may flourish. The teaching of grammatical forms will contribute essentially nothing to the improvement of children's speech habits.

Reliance on group instruction. The typical grade-school class follows an outline of study provided by a course of study, a textbook, or a work book. In the materials are lessons and drills for the correction of every conceivable type of error, regardless of whether or not the correction is needed by many, few, or none of the pupils, or even whether or not the supposed error is in need of correction. The teacher conscientiously follows the outline, spending many precious class hours on instruction and drill on language items requiring little or no attention for more than a few of the pupils. Indeed, in the case of pupils whose speech habits are already satisfactorily established, such instruction leads to confusion and doubt where none existed before.

Usage instruction should be as highly individualized as it is possible to make it. Only those errors least acceptable in the speech and writing of a majority of the class should be given class instruction and drill; those occurring in the work of a few should be handled in small groups or individually as the need arises. In all group work the attention of the class should be focused on the language activity for its own sake, rather than on the correction of errors. In this way the maximum class time can be given to positive, creative instruction in the uses of

[2] See Louis Zahner, *Language in General Education* (New York, D. Appleton-Century Company, Inc., 1940), Ch. III.

language, with time taken out only for those corrections requiring the attention of the entire class.

Reliance on "language periods." Although in the more progressive elementary schools instruction in language is highly integrated with all the subjects of instruction, finding expression in all the activities of the day's work, in the great majority of classrooms language exercises are programmed for a certain period of the day and are taught more or less in isolation from the normal language needs of the child in the total program. Thus it does occur that children are drilled in certain language corrections for thirty minutes in a "language period," yet are permitted to repeat the same error unchecked when using language for social studies, science, and other subjects. No amount of concentrated teaching can overcome the harmful effects of such lapses. The English language is not a subject to be taught and dropped; it is a series of skills to be established for all the needs of life. Correctness can only be established when it is maintained consistently and constantly, nor may lapses in the essential items be tolerated at any time. Stated more positively the principle is this: the habits and attitudes instilled by language instruction must function without lapse or deviation in every use of language throughout the school day, and so far as possible, in out-of-school hours. Only by unremitting watchfulness can old habits be broken and new ones established.

Reliance on work books and seat work. The great majority of language work books and seat-work practice pads are educationally unsound in both material and method. In material they are indiscriminate in selection of content and are far too inclusive for the ordinary needs of children. Side by side with fundamental correction, such as those given in List A above, appear rules and strictures of refinements beyond the needs of children, or rules based on ignorance and prejudice. Even were the type of practice given in such books the best aid to learning usage, there is in general insufficient practice on the fundamental items and far too much practice on unnecessary corrections.

The work books in language are generally unsound in method, in that the type of practice given is the filling in of blanks and the crossing out of alternate forms. Such practice may aid the brighter pupil to discover certain distinctions of usage, but it has very slight effect in the establishing of good habits or the breaking of undesirable habits. Such practice for the slower pupil often reinforces bad habits, as he tends to supply the familiar but undesirable form, or to cross off the desired form. Above all, such practice is futile because it is silent and detached from genuine communication. Usage practice must be heard and spoken to be effective, and it should always be in a setting of normal and natural use of language for a purpose recognized by the pupil.

A sound and successful program of teaching correct usage in the elementary grades can be built upon the understanding and application of three fundamental principles:

1. The teacher must size up the problem of correctness as it affects her class and plan a campaign to bring about specific results.

2. The pupils must be aroused to a desire to improve their usage, and coöperate actively with the teacher in striving toward the accomplishment of specific results.

3. Both teacher and pupils must consistently work at improved usage in the normal and natural uses of language

in the entire school program. This means no language exercises divorced from the purposes of communication; and no uses of communication, whatever the purposes, which ignore the claims of good usage.

With these principles assumed and made the directive force in the language instruction, the following procedures are recommended as leading to success in the goals of teaching good usage.

Teacher analysis of the problem. Within the first few weeks of school, teachers can easily prepare a list of the usage errors made by pupils in their classes. For younger children the list will be made by observation of their speech habits and a notation of the faults which appear. For older children this type of observation will still be necessary, but it can be reinforced by the analysis of errors appearing regularly in written language, not only in "compositions" but in the written work of the whole class program. These surveys will show which pupils make errors, what errors are made, and how frequently each error appears. When the surveys are completed, they should be checked against lists like those given on pages 180 and 181 in order to retain only the items which need concentrated attention in the grades.

The next step is to select from the list three or four of the most frequent and serious errors for the first line of attack. Where these errors and their corrections are made clear, the teacher will direct language activities to provide many opportunities to use the correct forms, and will be alert to permit no deviations or lapses from the correct forms at any time in the school day. When reasonable progress has been made in the correction of the first group of errors, the teacher will select the next three or four most important items and proceed toward their correction in the same manner.

Pupil interest in self-improvement. Unless a child really wants to improve his speech or writing, drill is a waste of time for him. Fundamental to all habit-forming is the conscious effort of the child to improve himself. Situations calling for the correct use of language should seem natural and real. Only a priggish child can be interested in talking or writing merely to improve his usage or to show the teacher that he has improved. If there is in a situation something that makes the pupil want to use language well, practice *in that situation* fixes the habits of good usage more solidly than large quantities of isolated drill.

If a talk is to inform or interest someone who does not know what the speaker is about to say, the pupil will feel that he has a reason for speaking well. Audience eagerness is a stimulus to effort. In addition to language activities arising from the daily instruction, such situations as introducing a visitor to the class, presenting a committee report, or making announcements in other rooms are all admirably suited to this purpose. Writing which has a goal in interested readers is more effective than daily composition exercises.[3] Children will practice untiringly to improve writing that may be published in a school newspaper. They will work hard to make accurate a letter that is actually to be mailed. The more social the class situation can be made, the more vital it will be to pupils.

Every effort should be made to place the responsibility for improvement upon the pupils themselves. They may

[3] See "Children Learn to Write," compiled by Fannie J. Ragland, Pamphlet No. 7, National Council of Teachers of English, 1944.

be encouraged to keep individual lists of the items which give them trouble; they will take great delight in crossing off the items which they have mastered to the satisfaction of the teacher and the class. Home coöperation may be secured through discussions in parent-teacher association meetings. Parents are usually eager to coöperate in language improvement when they know exactly what to do. Some teachers have used the device of having pupils write letters to their parents explaining the forms they are trying to use correctly and asking for reminders and help at home.

The development of language appreciation. It has been pointed out in Part I of this book that the correction of errors is only a part of instruction in good usage. Unfortunately, however, because of the prevalence of certain undesirable forms and the exceeding difficulty in their eradication, the correction of poor usage, which is after all only a negative kind of instruction, tends to overshadow and supplant more positive instruction leading to an appreciation of the ways of the English language. The child whose usage has been made reasonably "correct," but whose sentences are flat, dull, and inexact has not been taught good English usage. Language free from serious error is not necessarily good language. It becomes good as the child develops a feeling for the bright, sparkling word or phrase, the exact word for his needs, the sentence which says exactly what he wants to say as economically and clearly as possible. This feeling for the fitness of words in their uses is the positive side of usage instruction, the side to receive much more attention than has been given it. It is closely related, of course, to the development of effective speech and writing, and it can be taught well only in situations calling for genuine communication. Some suggestions for classroom procedure follow.

Enjoying words. Children find pleasure in the history of words, and are pleased to be told or to discover for themselves interesting facts about the words they use. Teachers can take advantage of words found in reading lessons, spelling lessons, composition, and class discussion to point out interesting facts. For example, there are fascinating stories behind such words as *daisy, window, lady, rival,* and so forth.[4] The words connected with holidays and other special occasions will interest children also. Where do we get such words as *Christmas, Easter, Noël;* the names of foods like *turkey, cranberry, sugar, punch, squash?* Exercises of this kind will arouse interest in words and will motivate attention to other word distinctions as the occasions arise.

Striving for the exact word. Unless spurred on to use the range of words that they know, children tend to employ a rather limited vocabulary in their speech and writing. The alert teacher will grasp every opportunity to encourage children to use less familiar words, and particularly to find the exact word needed to express a certain idea. Special exercises can be constructed to teach shades of meaning connected with a common idea. Take, for example, the verb *to go.* Ask the children to supply all the words they know that show a particular way of going. They will offer *stroll, saunter, skip, crawl, limp,* and many others. Let one child illustrate before the class the exact way of "going" expressed by each word. Then

---

[4] For information on these and other words the teacher is referred to Greenough and Kittredge, *Words and Their Ways in English Speech.*

discuss what kinds of people and what kinds of situations would probably be described by each word in the list. Finally, have stories told or written of trips taken by the pupils which would give occasion for many different verbs of motion. In class discussion following each talk or paper, let the children evaluate the effectiveness of the various verbs. Similar exercises can be constructed for such common ideas as *eat, look, say,* and *come.*

When the idea of exactness of meaning is established by exercises of this kind, the pupils should be encouraged in all talks and compositions to seek for the exact word which says better than any other the idea they wish to express. This type of positive approach to word selection will greatly enrich instruction in usage.

Recognizing the "social manners" of words. Every child knows without being told that some words are appropriate in one place but not in another. He realizes that some words are "taboo" and must not be uttered in public; he senses that some words are "elegant" and lend dignity to his speech when properly used. It is the task of usage instruction to increase the range of sensitivity to appropriateness in the use of words. What is the difference between "beat it" and "please go"? When is the right time to use each? When do you say "chuck the ball" and when "throw the ball"? What are the words used to invite a school friend to come in the house after school, and the words used to invite a grown-up friend of mother's to come in? Why is one set of words used for the first situation and another set for the second? When greeting someone you know, when is it appropriate to say "hi!" or "hello" or "how do you do"?

Discussions of this kind on the appropriateness of words will prepare pupils to be more sensitive to the appropriateness of words in their talks and papers. They should become alert to detect the inappropriate word in the speech or composition of a fellow-pupil and to know why the word is inappropriate. They will gradually come to appreciate the truth that words in themselves are not "right" or "wrong," but that the setting in which the word is used determines its correctness. This discovery is the foundation to a sound attitude toward usage. Children should be aided in making the discovery, and in applying it in all language situations in their school work. Increasing sensitivity to the fitness of words for specific uses is the ultimate goal of all usage instruction.

In the elementary grades language games will help to create sensitivity to the fitness of words. Some suggestions for games of this kind are made in Chapter XII, pp. 247-249.

X

The Teaching of Usage in the Junior High School

The principles stated in the preceding chapter for the teaching of usage in the elementary grades apply with equal force to the task in the junior high school. The differences in materials and methods between the elementary and junior high-school grades arise from the advance in the development of junior high-school pupils in mental maturity, range of interests, and command of language. In all but a few exceptional cases the language faults survived from baby-talk have been eliminated in the junior high-school pupil. He has gained sufficient acquaintance with the idiom of English to use pronouns in their various forms correctly, to form the tenses of the common regular and irregular verbs correctly, and to use plurals and possessives with reasonable accuracy. The faults which persist into the junior high-school years, or which develop in those years, are reflections of the language environment of the child outside of school. The seventh grader who has been exposed to consistently good English at home and at play speaks and writes correct colloquial English. In fact, his language use is in many cases superior to that of the average adult. The child who has been exposed to inferior English at home and at play persists in the faults which he constantly hears, through no fault of his own. Rarely is the influence of the elementary school strong enough to overcome the persistency of habits formed and reinforced in the home environment. The junior high school is in no better position to correct these faults by the influence only of the classroom. But the junior high school has a rare opportunity to enlist the pupil's active interest and co-operation in his own improvement, in those transition years from unself-conscious childhood to self-conscious adolescence.

For this reason the junior high-school grades are an especially critical period in a child's development. During these years when a child awakens to a social consciousness for the first time, habits may be readily formed or broken, ambitions aroused or crushed. If he can be led to understand that poor English usage habits are as detrimental to his social advancement as bad manners and untidy personal appearance, half the battle is won. There comes a time when every child begins voluntarily to wash behind his ears, comb his hair, clean his finger-nails, and black his shoes. The desire to im-prove his English may well be added to that list. But note that the combing of the hair, and other personal improvements, come about from the gradual develop-ment of a positive objective—to appear well among his fellows. The change is not the product of persistent rules, injunctions, and scoldings, as every mother knows. When the social objective is aroused, the changes take place automatically; until the objective is realized, external coercion is unheeded. It is important that the objective of good language use arise from a felt need for positive ends, rather than merely continued correction of faults.

Even the best will in the world, coupled with con-scientious instruction, will not work miracles over night.

A clear purpose, an intelligent program, and a saint-like patience are required of the teacher who would really influence the habits of children. A boy who was over-heard saying to a friend, "I ain't got no pencil; leave me take one of yours," turned shortly to his teacher to say, "I don't have a pencil. Please lend me one?" The problem, then, is not merely the teaching of the correct form, as in building up such an excellent classroom attitude toward good use as will permit no pupil to deviate from accepted patterns *because he respects the good opinion of his fellow-pupils.* The influence of such a social pressure once aroused by valid means, is more powerful than hours of conscientious practice and drill.

The principles, therefore, which underlie the attack on poor usage and the development of good usage in the junior high school may be summarized this way.

1. Limit the number of items to be studied and corrected so as to give emphasis where it is most needed.

2. Teach corrections soundly and reasonably, with oral practice, so as to gain group recognition of the error and group approval of the change to be made.

3. Teach usage positively so far as possible, to create a pattern of speech accepted by the class as an objective to work toward. The best way to break a bad habit is to substitute a better one in its place.

USAGE ITEMS FOR THE JUNIOR HIGH SCHOOL

To meet the first principle stated above, the limitation of items for specific attack to those of least acceptance and greatest need, the following list is suggested. Not all these items can be handled in any one year of the junior high-school course. Each teacher, after a careful inventory of the errors of speech and writing which occur in her class, should select from the list a reasonable number for careful teaching and drill. Obviously any items in this list which cause no trouble in the class, or which occur so infrequently as to be negligible in importance, should not be included in general class instruction. On the other hand, if certain errors from the list on page 180 persist with high frequency, then they should be included in the program.

I. ERRORS TO BE ATTACKED FOR ELIMINATION IN THE JUNIOR HIGH SCHOOL

  A. *Pronouns*

    1. Case forms

      a. Him, (her) and *me* went.

      b. It was *him, her, them.*

      c. Will you wait for John and *I?*

      d. Did you see her and *I?*

      e. Let him and *I* do the work.

      f. Us boys want to go.

      g. She invited *we* girls to the party.

      h. This is the man *which* did the work.

  B. *Verbs*

    1. Principal parts

      a. He *ask* me to go. (other *-ed* forms)

      b. They have *ate* all the melon.

      c. He has *began* to read the book.

      d. We *begun* the work at three o'clock.

      e. I have *broke* my pencil.

      f. I *brung* my lunch.

      g. My pencil is *busted.*

      h. He has *came* here before.

      i. He *done* the work well.

      j. I have *drank* all the milk.

      k. I *drunk* it all.

      l. She *give* me the picture.

      m. The bell has *rang.*

      n. He *run* all the way.

      o. Then he came to me and *says. ...*

      p. He *seen* the accident.

    q. My dress is *tore.*
    r. The boys have *went* home.
    s. My dress is *wore* out.
    t. I have *wrote* two letters.

2. Agreement with subject
    a. Her hair *are* long.
    b. One of the books *are* lost.
    c. Each of the books *are* interesting.
    d. He *don't* play tennis.
    e. There *is* two holidays this month.

3. Miscellaneous
    a. Jim *ain't* here now.
    b. Please *borrow* me a pencil.
    c. If he *had of* come, he would have built the fire.
    d. You *had* ought (*you'd* ought) to do that.
    e. He *laid* in the shade, *was laying* in the shade, wants to *lay* in the shade.
    f. *Learn* us a new game.
    g. *Leave* me see the butterfly.
    h. *Set* in this chair; he *set* in this chair, has *set* in this chair, etc.

C. *Adjectives and adverbs*
  1. Is he eating *a* apple?
  2. He writes *good.*
  3. This *here* book is mine.
  4. That *there* one is yours.
  5. Do you know *them* boys?
  6. I don't like *these kind* (*those kind,* or *sort*) of stories.

D. *Double negatives*
  1. He hasn't *neither* book.
  2. Haven't you *never* been to Chicago?
  3. Jane hasn't *no* pen.
  4. I haven't *nothing* to do.

E. *Miscellaneous*
  1. My brother *he* went to the football game. (and other double subjects)

While a great many of the forms listed in this outline will be taught as the need arises in composition, speech, reports, recitations, and so forth, some of them can be introduced or reinforced by instruction connected with grammar. For this reason they have been arranged in grammatical categories. But note well that from all the evidence available, *the study of grammar in itself has practically no effect on usage habits,* at least in the junior high school. When the child's desire to improve himself has been aroused, when certain specific faults have been made clear, and the desirable substitutes have been practiced, then he may be helped by a grammatical explanation of the fault and its correction. Grammatical reasons may strengthen changes already begun. However, it may be stated as an axiom for the junior high school: *grammar alone does not establish sound usage habits.*

In order to concentrate upon the forms most needed by junior high-school pupils, the teacher will have to neglect a variety of usage items which will ultimately need correction as the pupil matures. Outline II below is presented to suggest the type of usage deviations which may be ignored. Superior pupils whose usage has eliminated all errors in Outline I may be individually guided concerning items in Outline II. Such pupils tend to ask for such guidance and profit by corrections or suggestions made on compositions. The items in Outline II, however, will usually not receive class instruction in the junior high school. Indeed, many of them represent good current usage.

II. Forms to Receive No Class Instruction in the Junior High School

    A. *Pronouns*
       1. Case forms
          a. It is *me, us.*

  b. Tim is taller than *me, her, him.*
  c. Mary is as tall as *me, her, him.*
  d. Everybody (everyone) had *their* lesson.
  e. When *you* are driving a car *you* should be able to act quickly.
  f. Who did you invite?
  g. Who did you go with?
  h. Invite *whoever* you choose.

B. *Verbs*
 1. Agreement with subject
  a. The kind of games you like *are* too simple.
  b. Athletics *are* important in our school.
  c. Neither of the boys *are* here.
  d. Neither John nor George *are* here.
  e. The father with his two sons *were* here.
 2. Miscellaneous
  a. I guess I'll go.
  b. I haven't *got* any paints.
  c. I *got* home early.
  d. It *says* in my history book....
  e. I *will* probably go to the party.
  f. If I had time I *would* be glad to help you.

C. *Adjectives and adverbs*
 1. He's *awfully* rich.
 2. I feel *badly* about the accident.
 3. You walked *further* than I did.
 4. I am *kind of* tired.
 5. This is the *largest* of the two apples.
 6. *Most* anyone can do this work.
 7. I *only* saw her once.
 8. His work is *pretty* good.
 9. Come here *quick.*
 10. Drive *slow.*
 11. He's *sort of* angry.

D. *Conjunctions and prepositions*
 1. He isn't *as* tall as his brother.
 2. Divide the work *between* the four groups.
 3. Study your lesson *like* I do.

4. It looks *like* it will rain.
5. He fell off *of* the roof.
6. Your book is *different than* mine.

EFFECTIVE TEACHING PROCEDURES

To teach usage effectively in the junior high school, the following principles should be understood and applied in the planning of courses of study, the organizing of usage units, and the teaching of daily lessons. As an introduction to these principles it is suggested that the junior high-school teacher read the discussion of "popular fallacies in the teaching of usage" presented in Chapter IX.

PRINCIPLES FOR TEACHING USAGE
IN THE JUNIOR HIGH SCHOOL

1. Individualize instruction in usage so as to meet the most urgent needs of each pupil at the moment of his recognition of the need.

2. Emphasize desirable patterns of oral language, and by training the ear to be alert to language forms, assist the child in making his own corrections.

3. Place all usage instruction so far as possible in situations calling for the natural use of language in speech and writing.

4. Teach usage positively as well as negatively; develop sensitivity to appropriate forms of language for various needs in life.

Individualized instruction. To the teacher in the typical junior high school meeting five or six classes a day with an average of thirty pupils to a class, the idea of individualized teaching in usage may seem preposterous. Yet with a clear notion of the goals to be reached, a strategic plan of action, and some materials worked out in advance, any teacher can individualize instruction in usage to a considerable degree. The following steps will show how to organize for such instruction.

Diagnosis. It is essential to know at the outset the distribution of pupils in any class into these three groups: (1) those who have adequate command of ordinary colloquial English, and whose errors, if any, will be in matters beyond the needs of the class as a whole; (2) those who are reasonably accurate, but lapse into error through carelessness or as the result of out-of-school influences; (3) those who need a great deal of instruction and practice to overcome faulty habits, and sometimes to overcome undesirable attitudes toward usage.

There are three sources of information readily obtained in making an analysis of a class. The first source is a usage test, either one created by the teacher to test usage items such as those in Outline I on page 194 above, or a published test which may be purchased. Chapter XII contains sample tests of the kind which teachers may make, and also a list of recommended published tests. When the test has been administered and corrected, the pupils' scores will give the first source of information toward grouping the class.

The second source of information from the class is written composition. To be valid the composition, or a series of compositions, should be written in class. The subjects chosen should be lively and interesting, so as to secure the maximum of free, natural expression from the children. Their attention should be centered on the content of the composition, not on the form. With such spontaneous writing, the normal language habits of the children will emerge: some will write fluently and accurately, some will write fluently and very inaccurately, some will be painstakingly careful, others will be grossly careless, and so forth. From such a composition or compositions, the teacher may determine fairly well the level of accuracy of each child, and also the typical usage errors of the group.

The third immediate source of information is speech. Having set up a situation in which each child may speak freely and naturally, and with his attention centered on what he wants to say rather than on the form or correctness of his speech, the teacher will record on a card for each pupil the types of speech errors which occur, and the relative frequency of error for each child. The first observation will be only reasonably accurate, since the level of children's speech is influenced by a number of factors. But repeated observations, checked against the same record card, should render a fairly reliable index of the pupils' normal speech habits, and the diagnosis of particular difficulties through their repetition.

For the recording of data from these sources, a chart or record sheet is recommended, of the type illustrated here.

LANGUAGE USAGE ANALYSIS

Pupils' Name	Test Results Percentile Score	Written Composition	Speech Habits	Group Assignment
Adams, Jane ..	90	Accurate	Excellent	I
Bell, Addison .	50	Sometimes inaccurate	Fair	II
Conrad, Peter.	20	Very poor	Many Errors	III
Davis, Joan ..	65	Fair	Unreliable	II?
Edgar, Lou...	45	Unreliable	Fair	III?

Administrative procedures. In the periods devoted expressly to usage instruction and practice, the members of Group I should be excused from the class activity and permitted to read, write, or carry out any other self-directed activity as assigned by the teacher. It should be clear to the pupils that continued membership in Group I is a privilege to be maintained by consistent accuracy in writing and speech, and by efficient use of the time freed from class work.

Groups II and III will follow the pattern of instruction as set by the teacher, with blackboard practice, textbook exercises, and work sheets. Pupils tentatively placed in Group II who are consistently able to perform the exercise work with reasonable accuracy should be moved into Group I, also tentatively, until they prove their ability to be self-reliant in usage.

Materials of instruction. Published work books may be used for usage practice provided they have been chosen after careful study to be sure that the content of the exercises is suitable to the grade level. It is also wise to go through each exercise before assigning it for practice, to discard those items which are too advanced for the class, or which are based on false standards of usage. For example, in a work-book exercise for the seventh grade on the uses of the verb *to be*, these two items stand side by side:

21. I was certain that you (was, were) there.
22. If it (was, were) only true!

Item 21 presents a basic error which social usage demands to be corrected. Item 22 presents the subjunctive of condition contrary to fact, a literary distinction of no basic importance to the seventh grade. Such an item should be canceled out before the pupils begin work. Because of this indiscriminate mixing of usage levels in exercises, most work books are unreliable and are losing favor with conscientious teachers.

Many teachers prefer to make their own practice sheets, since by so doing they meet more adequately the needs of their own pupils. When carefully designed and duplicated by mechanical means, each exercise sheet may be used for a number of years, since the pupils write the answers on their own papers or in notebooks. The great advantages of such sheets are that any particular one may be used at any time to help a backward pupil, to practice a point arising in composition, or to help an absent pupil make up back work. Moreover, with such sheets pupils may work at their own rates, bringing the completed exercise to the teacher for correction and approval.

The implied principles in this section on individualized instruction in usage are: (1) no pupil should be required to practice and drill on usage items which he has already mastered. (2) Every pupil should have a personal incentive to raise himself to a higher group position. (3) Those who need most practice and drill should be able to repeat basic exercises without holding back their classmates.

Oral language. There is a great difference between allowing children to talk and developing sound habits of speech. Unfortunately this difference is not sufficiently recognized. Let it be stated here clearly: the act of talking in itself does not improve the quality of speech. Speech is improved only when teacher and pupil are conscious of definite goals and strive together toward their attainment.

Educators of the liberal stamp have been stressing in recent years the importance of releasing the junior high-school classroom from rigid restraint, silent seat work, and formal recitations, in order to create a social atmosphere of freedom in which teacher and pupils can chat together over their common interest. Such freedom has increased greatly the opportunity for the use of oral language in its most natural forms. But the caution stated in the preceding paragraph must be kept in mind. Increasing the quantity of talk does not increase its quality unless definite steps are taken to set standards and to maintain them through vigilance on the part of teacher and pupils. Even while such vigilance is essential, it must not become the source of embarrassment and self-consciousness, or else all the value of free communication will be lost. Some suggestions for preserving freedom while improving speech are offered in the following typical classroom activities.

Recitation. Despite the good intentions of well-meaning teachers, there is still far too much monosyllabic recitation permitted or even encouraged in junior high-school classrooms. This observation applies to classes in social studies, science, and mathematics as well as to classes in English. In a recitation heard recently the children had finished reading an account of Luther Burbank and were ready to talk about it. There was keen interest and lively response—in this form. *Teacher*: "What was Luther Burbank called?" *Class*: in chorus: "The plant wizard!" *Teacher*: "Where did he do his work?" *Class*: "California!" *Teacher*: "What was one of his earliest discoveries?" *Class*: "Burbank potato!" and so on for about fifteen minutes. Not a single child formulated a whole sentence to tell what he knew about Burbank. Children must have the opportunity constantly to express themselves in full statements, for two reasons: the full statement, clearly made, reveals beyond all doubt the child's grasp of the fact, idea, or principle which was being taught; and second, the full statement gives practice in the positive side of usage—the combining of words at will to communicate meaning effectively and appropriately.

These simple rules, if followed faithfully, will insure the sound use of recitation as the means of teaching the subject of the lesson; the skill of communication, and good language usage simultaneously.

1. Insist upon full statements in grammatical sentences.

2. Let the class check the statements for clarity and accuracy. Let other pupils improve faulty statements by making better statements.

3. Correct usage errors instantly. There may be justification for permitting an error to pass unchecked in a formal talk, but there is no excuse in recitation. Insist on good language use, but don't be fussy.

4. Help the hesitant student to find a sentence pattern for his needs. Good sentences come from practice, not inspiration. Start the hesitant student, but be sure that he makes a full statement himself and does not merely add to the start you have given him.

Discussion. A great part of junior high-school instruction is conducted by means of organized or free discussion. In organized discussion there is a chairman who recognizes the speakers, keeps the class to the point, and directs the outcome of the discussion. The chairman is frequently the teacher, perhaps too frequently, for junior high-school pupils are quite competent to preside over organized discussion. In free discussion pupils talk without the leadership of a chairman, and without raising hands to be recognized. This latter type is most fruitful in training children to talk freely and naturally, but it must follow adequate training in the courtesies of group speech. Free discussion becomes essentially conversation, and follows the practices observed by polite people when gathered in a group. A few simple principles apply to discussion:

1. Present one fact, idea, as illustration at a time.

2. Speak briefly and wait for someone to reply.

3. Never interrupt a speaker; or if one has accidentally interrupted, apologize and wait till the speaker has finished.

4. Refer to previous speakers by name in answering questions or arguments.

The teacher should remain in the background as much as possible, but she is justified in interrupting to ask for a full statement, or to ask a pupil to correct himself when he has misrepresented fact or misused normal conversational English. While the talk should remain free and natural, the ends of good speech are defeated if gross errors of correctness are permitted to pass unchecked. A courteous request to the student to rephrase his statement will remind the pupils that the teacher is vigilant, and will help them to become so.

Short talks. The commonest device for promoting practice in oral language is the short prepared talk. Because the pupil is before an audience and is therefore the center of attention, errors of good use may be permitted to pass unchecked at the moment if the correction will embarrass the pupil or put him off his stride. But at the close of the talk the more serious errors should be brought to his attention *by the teacher,* and so far as is possible he should be led to restate the sentences in which the errors occurred.

It is common practice in many classrooms to let the pupils criticize the errors of language of their classmates. This practice is undesirable for two important reasons: first, watching for errors takes attention away from the content of the talk and centers it on the language, defeating the purposes of communication. Second, the pupils are unable to discriminate properly in the sort of errors they criticize; they tend to criticize everything the least bit unfamiliar, and overlook the commonest errors. In oral talks the best procedure is to lead pupils to evaluate the content of a classmate's talk, and comment on its success as communication. When this evaluation is completed, then the teacher may call attention to language faults, if any, and encourage the pupil to recast the faulty sentences before he takes his seat.

Natural settings for language. In the preceding section it has been pointed out that a great part of junior high-school instruction is conducted by means of recitation, discussion, and short reports. These situations are by far the best setting for instruction in oral language, since the talk has a purpose, and the attention of the children is focused on the content for its own sake, as the attention ought to be in all good communication. It is regrettable that the use of language books in junior high-school English classes leads to artificiality in the motivation of language. The class which has just seen an absorbing experiment in science, or has discussed a leading problem in social studies, or has witnessed a motion picture in the school auditorium, is too often forced to put such *real* motivation out of mind in order to read some silly little story in a language text as the basis for discussion and oral practice. Even worse, the exercise may consist entirely of correcting verbs, pronouns and the like in sentences manufactured for the purpose, having no relationship to the children's interests and needs, and performing no function of communication whatever. The conscientious teacher of English will be alert to use natural settings for spoken exercises and will teach correctness, good usage, and good manners in oral English through and by means of the subjects and topics which the children *really want to talk about.*

The same principle applies to written work. Every child should have the opportunity to express himself freely on paper at frequent intervals. The subjects of writing should arise as much as is possible from the experiences of the day which have stimulated him— experiences in school or out of school. The language text-book cannot (or at least does not) provide this natural motivation. It tends to present stereotyped situations with smug little models to be studied and imitated. Free expression of ideas, free choice of subject, natural moti-vation, and pride of individual achievement are all lost in such formalized teaching. The concept of good usage is more than avoiding mistakes, as has been repeatedly stated in this book. It is the use of language for genuine communication of personal ideas—language which effi-ciently and appropriately says what the author wants to say. Artificial exercises will often result in accuracy, but it is fair to ask, accuracy for what purpose? A child has mastered good usage only when language meets his own needs to say well what he wants to communicate to others. For this reason, the more often composition arises from the real needs of the pupil to communicate, the more often he is developing competence in handling language effectively for after-school purposes.

Teach usage positively. The final principle in teaching good usage to junior high-school pupils is to teach in such a manner that the pupil's powers of communication expand rather than contract. The rules of games like tennis and checkers are not imposed to hamper the play but to make purposeful play possible. Even young children can see that tennis is more than a random batting of balls over a net, and checkers more than the idle sliding of counters across a board. The good teacher of either game does not stress the restrictions but teaches patiently the positive moves. The restrictions arise incidentally as the learner masters the technique. The analogy of games may be applied without violence to the teaching of usage. The purpose of language is to communicate, not to learn rules, just as the purpose of tennis is to play a game. The rules guide the play and impose restrictions *for the sake of the play* but a player who delays the game to be fussy over rules is exceedingly unpopular. In like fashion the rules of usage must be taught to expedite communication, but never to get in its way.

If this point seems to be labored too strongly, look at the evidence. In a recent survey of the teaching of English [1] in a midwestern state in something over 500 classrooms engaged in language lessons, approximately 9 out of 10 classes were correcting usage in notebooks, work books, or language texts, in sentences having no significance to the children, and forming no part of the natural communication of children. In the tenth classroom the children were learning language by writing or speaking and by correcting and improving *their own language difficulties*. Isolated language drills may sometimes be justified for practice, but they fail of their purpose if they are not followed immediately by some type of communication on the part of the student to show that he has mastered the drill material in his own self-directed language.

A seventh-grade teacher complained recently, "I can't let the children write their own stories. They make too

[1] "The Language Arts Survey in Wisconsin Elementary Schools," *Elementary English Review* (January, 1946), pp. 8-14.

many mistakes." So she discussed a story with the children, phrased sentences which she wrote on the blackboard, and then set the children to work copying it! The bulletin board in this same room had fourteen composition papers displayed, all containing a story told in identical words. What was displayed was penmanship, not language skill. Instruction of this kind will produce neat papers, it is true, but it does next to nothing to develop independent command of language.

SUGGESTIONS FOR THE CONSTRUCTIVE TEACHING OF ENGLISH USAGE

Praise each well-phrased sentence. In recitation, discussion, or oral talks, the teacher should be alert to catch a well-turned sentence, an explanation made clear by a well-chosen word, or a touch of humor in the turn of a phrase. When such sentences occur in recitation or discussion, they should be praised at once, quietly and sincerely. Children are quick to catch the genuine approbation of the teacher, and they are more pleased by it than they frequently show. Recognition by the teacher of good phrasing will encourage greater effort by the pupils to speak well, for children almost universally try to do what the teacher wants. A chief cause of poor classroom expression is the failure of teachers to expect and require anything better.

Encourage experimentation with words. Junior high-school pupils are at the age when the expansion of vocabulary is great. Through the richness of experience of the junior high-school curriculum they should be adding new words to their vocabularies at a rapid rate. If encouraged to use these words they will do so, but it is inevitable that they will make mistakes in pronunciation and appropriateness. The mistake is innocent, but if it brings down rebuke or ridicule on the pupil, or even an ironic correction from the teacher, the whole spirit of experimentation with words is destroyed. Watch for new words and praise them, even when mistakenly used. A correction made with praise for the attempt will encourage future attempts. In a seventh-grade class a boy was reporting on the harbor of New York City. "After passing the Statue of Liberty," he said, "we came to Ellis Island, where the migratories are landed." A laugh at his expense for the word *migratories* might have crushed something good in this pupil. But the teacher seized on the word, showed how the boy had chosen the correct root meaning, pointed out the analogy between migrating people and migrating birds, and finally substituted the word *immigrants*. The class was impressed, the boy was pleased and the spirit of word experimentation was fostered.

Correct errors constructively. When asking for certain written work from a pupil, the teacher received this by no means uncommon reply, "I didn't have no time to do it." The pupil who replies thus is almost never deliberately misusing English. On the contrary, he is following the most natural of language phenomena, unconsciously reflecting the speech patterns of his environment. No haphazard or irritated correction will help the child. The best response would be something like, "John, can you tell me that in a better way?" If he can correct himself, good; if not, another pupil may be asked to help him. But John must himself rephrase the statement before the matter is dropped. This procedure takes time, it is true, but time and patience are the very essence of language correction. In what better way could time be spent than helping John correct himself, and impressing on the class the importance of accurate usage?

Give public approval to good writing. In the correction and evaluation of written work, the teacher should be constantly on the watch for the successful wording of an idea. It may be the accurate employment of a new word, the concise phrasing of a comparison, or the successful use of emphasis or antithesis. Form the habit of marking such passages, with the comment, "Good!" or "Fine phrase!" in the margin. Read aloud phrases, sentences, and even whole paragraphs of this type to the class. If possible get the pupils to tell why the passage is unusually good; if they are unable to do so, tell them why it has been selected. Such notice and praise will encourage the writer to greater efforts, will show the class what you want, and will keep uppermost in the minds of the pupils the importance of accurate and interesting wording.

Post well-written composition. Written composition is on display in surprisingly few classrooms. Yet the bulletin board is an excellent means to stimulate interest in better self-expression. Post a few compositions at a time—not always those with the best penmanship—but select some in which unusually good phrasing is apparent, as in which a particular word may be spotted by a circle, with the comment "Good!" Junior high-school pupils in general try to produce what the teacher wants; low aim, not failure is too often our crime.

Discuss inaccurate or inappropriate wording from pupils' compositions. A very good seventh-grade pupil wrote an original story about a mother duck and her first hatched egg—her fears and joys as her little one appeared from the shell. His wording was simple and sincere. Then came his final sentence: "The mother cuddled her little one closer, while the sun sank flaming into the sea." There had been no previous mention of the sun, nor was time an element of the story. The teacher raised the query as to the appropriateness of the final sentence. The class discussed the matter, and led the writer into making his own decision that a florid ending of this sort was not appropriate to the simplicity of his story. It really spoiled the effect of sincerity which he had earlier achieved.

This type of analysis and discussion is an excellent way to teach the positive side of good usage. Unfortunately, the procedure is very rare in English classrooms.

Help pupils to observe the levels of speech about them. Junior high-school pupils enjoy making observations leading to reports. Send them out to make notes on the speech of members of the community (but never members of their own families). The best observations are made of strangers or anonymous representatives of the community. The report should describe the type of person observed, his probable occupation and employment, the place of observation, the characteristics of the speech of the subject, and the pupil's evaluation of his speech.

A number of reports of this type, discussed in class by the pupils, preferably without judgments from the teacher, will lead the pupils to be conscious of types and levels of speech in their community, and the importance of appropriate choices in speech for particular occasions.

Summary. Good usage is more than correcting errors. Teach usage positively as much as possible; make it interesting and meaningful. The improved attitude of pupils toward speech correction and accurate writing will go far to eliminate the errors which must be constantly corrected.

XI

The Teaching of Usage in the
Senior High School

THE PROBLEM

Teaching correct usage in the senior high school is definitely the continuation of skills, attitudes, and habits properly begun in the kindergarten and developed through the grades and the junior high school. In no phase of English instruction is the sense of continuous growth and progress more important to teachers and pupils than in the teaching of correct usage. Good habits developed in earlier years must be maintained, persisting faults must be analyzed and corrected as in the earlier grades, and new problems arising from the greater demands of senior high-school speaking and writing must be approached from techniques and attitudes previously formed. For these reasons it is recommended that senior high-school teachers read Chapter IX, "Foundations in the Elementary Grades," and Chapter X, "The Teaching of Usage in the Junior High School" before reading this chapter, in order to gain a conception of the continuous and developmental nature of usage teaching. Moreover, many of the techniques recommended for usage teaching in the junior high school apply with equal validity to the task of the senior high school. In truth, the retarded senior high-school pupil is on the instructional level of the normal junior high-school pupil, and can profit from a continuation of the teaching procedures recommended for grades seven, eight and nine.

In the senior high school the teaching of usage is a two-fold responsibility. One part is remedial, the correction of errors that persist from earlier years, and the correction of new errors which arise from increased use of language at a higher level. The other part is constructive, the teaching of effective patterns of speech for wider needs, and the refinement of word-choice to increase the interest and effectivness of expression. Because the remedial aspect is the more apparent need and is in nature more concrete, it tends to supplant or overshadow the constructive responsibility.

That many of the most flagrant errors in English usage still persist in the informal speech and in the written work of the boys and girls he teaches is distressingly evident to the high-school teacher of English. Frequently the problem of raising the usage level of his pupils is so baffling that he is overwhelmed with discouragement. When the problem is analyzed, however, it is simplified somewhat, for only a relatively small number of really gross errors are both widespread and frequent. One hundred sixty teachers in Wisconsin high schools rated the following errors as the ten most serious occurring among their pupils (see table on next page).

It is significant that, although these gross errors—belonging indisputably on the illiterate level of usage—have been corrected throughout the first nine grades, they still remain the most frequent errors in grades ten, eleven, and twelve.

In spite of the persistence of error and the remedial steps necessary to bring about improvement in usage, the high-school program in language development must not be looked upon as purely corrective. Language in-

Ten Most Serious Errors

Error	Number of Teachers Reporting It
Double negative	70
ain't got no	
haven't no	
didn't have nothing	
I seen it	56
this here	56
the boy he	55
he ain't	46
I done it	44
leave him go	35
you was	28
hair are	27
would of seen [1]	26

Items submitted by Wisconsin teachers to a committee of the Wisconsin English Association in 1932-33.

struction in the senior high school must be focused upon the constant expansion of powers to use language effectively for the needs of school and life after school. To this end the major portion of time in the English course should be given to two types of constructive activities:

1. Guided practice in oral language by means of reports, discussions, panels, forums, debates, and extemporary dramatics. These exercises should be conducted so as to provide opportunities for every pupil to take an active part at frequent intervals, and to make growth in effectiveness of oral presentation through the guidance of the teacher and the suggestions of his fellow-pupils.

2. Constant growth in written language by means of composition exercises at regular and frequent intervals. These written exercises should cover a wide range of subjects, with the time allotment fairly equally divided between two types of writings: (a) factual-expository writing, as in reports, summaries, explanations, arguments, and editorials; and (b) personal-imaginative writing, as in the relation of personal

[1] Written substitute for would've.

experiences, essays, narratives, fantasy, humor, and in some cases, drama and poetry.

In this constructive program of language development correctness plays an essential but subordinate part. Every language exercise, oral and written, should have an intrinsic purpose of its own, a purpose recognized by the pupil and ideally one which challenges him to do his best. Good usage and the correction of error should be seen as contributory to the accomplishment of the purpose of the exercise, not ends in themselves. Indeed, the best instruction in correctness at the high-school level is that which arises naturally from the needs of the pupils as they strive to accomplish effective expression for a definite purpose. Such instruction makes sense and finds immediate application in the task at hand. Specific suggestions for constructive usage teaching will be found on pp. 235-240, as well as on pp. 209-213.

USAGE ITEMS FOR THE SENIOR HIGH SCHOOL

It has been the consistent point of view of this book that successful teaching of usage depends upon limiting the items of instruction at each level to those of greatest need. The following outlines represent the application of this principle to the senior high school. The errors in Outline I are those which large numbers of teachers have reported as persisting in high-school years in spite of earlier instruction, or growing out of the expanded expressional needs of the senior high-school pupil. Because of the potential relationship between correctness of usage and instruction in grammar at the high-school level, the items have been grouped according to grammatical categories, and are arranged in alphabetical order within the categories.

High-school teachers will find this list chiefly useful

in two ways. First, it provides a check list for the analysis of pupils' speech and composition. Errors occurring frequently in the language exercises of pupils which are found also in this list can be safely taken as essential items for instruction and practice in the usage program. Secondly, this list may be used to check against exercises in textbooks and work books. Items on this outline should receive major emphasis in any practice exercises. Items not on this outline may be disregarded or passed over lightly. For example, some textbook exercises give as much attention to practice in "It is I" as in "It is he, she." Because society tolerates "It's me" but does not tolerate "It's him, her" the wise teacher will strike out the "It is I" exercises before assigning the practice, in order to give major consideration to the items socially important to correct. This same principle applies to the other grammatical categories.

I. ERRORS TO BE ATTACKED FOR ELIMINATION IN THE SENIOR HIGH SCHOOL

   A. *Pronouns*

      1. Case forms

         a. It was her, him, them.[2]

         b. I am as tall as him, her, or taller than him, her.

         c. Did you see John and I?

         d. Give the book to John or I.

         e. Let him and I go.

         f. Everyone came but she and John; or, John and I.

         g. Us fellows went early.

         h. The candy was meant for we girls.

      2. Agreement with antecedent

         a. Everybody brought their friends.

---

[2] The only exceptions which usage makes to the pattern of the nominative following the verb, *to be* are "It is me" and the less frequent "It is us."

      b. Has everyone their hats?
      c. Everyone helped themselves.
      d. He is the one which did it.

B. *Verbs*

1. Principal parts
    a. The fender is broke.
    b. He begun the work early.
    c. Has the mail came?
    d. He come early.
    e. He has did the work well.
    f. I done the work alone.
    g. He has drank all of the water.
    h. I drunk the pop.
    i. The water was froze.
    j. He give me the book.
    k. Has the bell rang?
    l. He run a mile.
    m. Have you saw the movie?
    n. He handed me the letter and says. . . .
    o. I seen it last night.
    p. He is suppose to go. (and other -d forms)
    q. We have went three times.
    r. He has wrote the letter.

2. Agreement with subject
    a. Either Jack or Ed are going.
    b. One of these sports are especially popular.
    c. My hair are straight.
    d. It don't matter when we go.
    e. Every one of the boys have come.
    f. She is one of those girls who is easily offended.
    g. There is several magazines on the table.
    h. We, you, they, Jim and Henry was there.

3. Miscellaneous
    a. Fred ain't here now.
    b. Will you borrow me a pencil? [3]
    c. She et her lunch.
    d. He had ought (hadn't ought) to go.

[3] This misuse of *borrow* is common in certain parts of Wisconsin.

    e. If he had of come, he would have had a good time.

    f. He lays down, laid down, was laying down, has laid down, wants to lay down, etc.

    g. Learn us the game.

    h. Leave him go now.

    i. The river raised last night.

    j. Let me set at the head table.

    k. If he would have done the work, he wouldn't have failed.

    l. If he hadn't studied, he would of failed.[4]

C. *Adjectives and adverbs*
1. I am a admirer of art.
2. He does his work good.
3. This here pencil is broken.
4. That there pen scratches.
5. These kind (those kind or sort) of books don't appeal to me.
6. Them books are all yours.

D. *Double negatives*
1. She can't hardly carry a tune.
2. I haven't hardly any paper.
3. We haven't never been late before.
4. He hasn't no book of his own.
5. They haven't nothing to do now.

E. *Miscellaneous*
1. Where is the party at?
2. That is all the farther (further) I went.
3. Then this man he tried to escape. (and other double subjects)

The expressions that follow in Outline II are either established in present usage or are still in dispute. If the forms are established, there can be no reason for trying to correct them; if they are in dispute, few pupils have time to bother with them. A more favorable attitude

---

[4] *Would of* is, of course, an error that occurs only in writing. The oral elision, *would've*, appears frequently in the conversation of educated people.

toward good English can be created by concentrating attention upon a relatively small number of language forms. A few defects may be cured, but to be told that nearly all of one's language habits are bad is merely discouraging. Although the forms in the following list do not deserve class attention, individuals who inquire about any of them should certainly be given as accurate information as possible and should be urged to observe how the forms are used. They may be told that an expression is acceptable for colloquial but not for more formal English, that even for colloquial use a given form seems to be preferred, or that no preference can be indicated.

II. FORMS TO RECEIVE NO CLASS INSTRUCTION IN THE SENIOR HIGH SCHOOL

   A. *Pronouns*
      1. Case forms
         a. It is me.
         b. Who did you invite?
         c. Who is it for? [5]
         d. I will work with whoever you suggest.

      2. Agreement with antecedent
         a. They had a bad earthquake in San Francisco last week.
         b. Everyone was here, but they all went home early.[6]
         c. I failed to answer his question, which was thoughtless of me.

[5] For colloquial use the interrogative *who* may be used instead of *whom* unless the pronoun in the sentence follows immediately its verb, verbal, or preposition. The relative *whom* presents practically no problem because of the common tendency to omit the pronoun or to use *that*, e.g., "a girl I know," "a girl that I know."

[6] The plural pronoun may have a singular antecedent if in the sentence the pronoun is far removed from its antecedent, especially if the plural idea is very strong. If the pronoun is placed near its antecedent, good usage follows the grammatical rule for agreement, e.g., "Everyone brought his friends."

        d. If you are going to make a windmill, you need tools.[7]

  3. Unclassified
    a. They invited my guests and myself.

B. *Verbs*

  1. Agreement with subject [8]
    a. Athletics are stressed in most schools.
    b. The kind of tools you want are hard to find.
    c. Neither of the boys were here.
    d. None were willing to oppose the bill.

  2. Miscellaneous
    a. I've got to write the letter.
    b. I got home early.
    c. I will probably be at the party.[9]
    d. Will you want this book tonight?
    e. I would go if I were you.
    f. Would you go if I stayed at home?
    g. He said that New York was a large city.[10]

C. *Adjectives and adverbs*

  1. It was awfully kind of you to come.
  2. I feel badly.
  3. He ran further than I did.
  4. Most everyone came.
  5. I only have fifty cents.
  6. Come quick.
  7. It is pretty cold today.
  8. The wind is real strong.
  9. You'd better drive slow.

[7] In informal speech and writing, the indefinite *you* is permissible. It also appears frequently in literary English.

[8] There is an increasing tendency for a verb to agree with the meaning rather than with the form of the subject.

[9] Very little distinction is made between the uses of *shall* and *will* and *should* and *would*. "Shall I," however, is regarded as being more courteous than "Will I?"

[10] Such attraction to the past tense is common and probably established.

D. *Conjunctions and prepositions*

1. He isn't as old as Henry.
2. The reason he wrote a poor test was because he was ill.
3. Arrangements were made to divide the work between the four girls.
4. I don't know if I can go.
5. It looks like it would rain.
6. I tried to swing the racket like you do.[11]

E. *Miscellaneous*

1. Try and finish the work on time.
2. What was the reason for Henry objecting? [12]
3. He tried to thoroughly understand the problem.[13]

ENGLISH USAGE AND ENGLISH GRAMMAR

It is a common complaint of high-school teachers, particularly teachers of English, Latin, and modern foreign languages, that pupils coming from the grades or junior high school do not know any grammar. Contrary to popular opinion, this condition of ignorance is as it should be: children in the grades, and those of the junior high school in grades seven and eight have no need of grammatical analysis, nor are they mentally equipped to profit from grammatical instruction. It is a sad fact that the time now spent in grades five to eight inclusive in attempting to establish grammatical principles actually

[11] *Like* for *as* or *as if* is generally permitted in conversation and informal writing but not for formal use.

[12] Either the possessive or accusative case of a noun seems to be accepted before a gerund. The accusative case of a pronoun in this position is open to dispute.

[13] The split infinitive is permissible except when the use of it produces an awkward construction.

impedes rather than advances development in communication.[14]

The reasons commonly advanced for teaching grammar prior to grade nine are:

1. Grammar is an important body of knowledge to be taught regardless of its practical value.

2. Grammar improves correctness of usage in speaking and writing.

3. Grammar improves sentence structure and variety of expression.

4. Grammar (English grammar) is essential to the study of Latin, French, German, and so forth.

How valid are these reasons? Very few teachers will today defend the first reason, though in fact it may be the soundest, or at least the most honest, of the four. The second reason may have some validity in the upper high-school years; it has none at all in the grades and junior high school. There is no evidence to show that the study of parts of speech, subjects, verbs, and so forth, influences in any significant way the speech and writing habits of children under 14 years of age. Grammar supports usage at the point when the child can grasp a generalization and apply it accurately to particulars. This ability implies a maturity of reasoning processes rarely reached by a ninth-grade pupil. Children's language is and should be the product of habits; good habits should be encouraged and continued, bad habits should be checked and replaced by better habits. In this process of habit formation the application of reason,

[14] For a discussion of grammar in modern education, see Louis Zahner and Others, *Language in General Education* (New York, D. Appleton-Century Company, Inc., 1940), Ch. III. See also, W. V. Kaulfers, *The Teaching of Grammar* (Stanford University, Calif., Stanford Book Store, 1945).

such as the explanation of the tenses of verbs, the case and number of pronouns, and the grammatical construction of sentences, contributes very slightly indeed to the formation of better habits in children. The time spent in grammar teaching would be more profitably used in the actual practice of writing and speaking, where the new habits to be formed would find direct application and immediate use.

The third reason, that grammar improves sentence structure, is probably valid for those elements of grammar which bear directly upon the structure of sentences. Below grade nine the only parts of grammar contributing directly to sentence sense are the subject and the verb. While no specific evidence in objective form is available, it is reasonable to assume that pupils will write more sentences containing a subject and a verb if they know what subjects and verbs are and can identify them *in their own sentences*. In grade nine and above the further analysis of the sentence into clauses, and the addition of the verbal phrases (participle, infinitive, gerund) provides all the grammar that the student will find necessary to bring variety and clarity into sentence structure.

That English grammar is essential to the teaching of Latin and foreign languages is no valid reason for burdening the junior high-school curriculum with formal grammar. Language teachers are bound by the same traditional fallacy apparent in much English teaching— they are attempting to teach the facts of the structures of their languages before the pupil has developed any desire to communicate in the language. When the pupil wants to read, write, or speak effectively in the foreign tongue, he will be ready for, and eager to accept the grammatical explanations which make his task easier. The improved teaching of languages developed in the war years will do much to eliminate the demand for categorical English grammar as a prerequisite to the study of foreign tongues.

In summary then: high-school teachers of the ninth grade should expect no more grammar of pupils entering their classes than the ability to recognize subjects and verbs, the ability to write a correctly constructed simple sentence, and the ability to analyze a simple sentence into subject and predicate. Further development of the sentence is the task of the senior high school. From the angle of good usage, the ninth-grade teacher should expect evidences of *much practice in speaking and writing* with emphasis on accuracy in speaking and writing skills. In the senior high school the grammar of tense, case, number, and agreement may be taught to explain the reasons for certain usage choices ("taller than *I*," "for *whom*," between you and *me*") provided the time spent on grammar does not reduce in any way the continuous practice of speaking and writing, and provided each grammatical exercise finds *immediate application* in a practical language situation. Some such situations are suggested later in this chapter.

EFFECTIVE TEACHING PROCEDURES

It is not uncommon for errors of usage on the senior high-school level, particularly those errors which persist in spite of repeated corrective drill, to be ascribed to "carelessness." To dismiss pupils' errors as "careless" may relieve the feelings of the teacher, who in this way shifts the responsibility to the pupils, but to use the term does not explain why pupils go so persistently wrong when it would seem no more difficult for them to be occasionally right. In the use of the adjective "careless" a clear distinction should be made between errors of mechanical accuracy and errors of word-choice. The failure to place periods, question marks, quotation marks, and other signs of punctuation in written work; the failure to indent for paragraphs, or to capitalize proper nouns may in most cases in the senior high school be ascribed to carelessness. The offenders have not learned, or do not apply what they have learned. But word-choice, grammatical unity, and idiomatic syntax are in a different category. Here the child who errs is almost always reflecting language habits formed before school years, and strengthened by constant repetition in the home environment. The key to any measure of success in overcoming the force of environment in such cases lies in the creation of two desirable attitudes rather than upon intensity of drill. The first attitude is that of willingness on the part of the pupil to recognize that some of his speech habits are undesirable and his consent to a voluntary program of self-improvement. The second attitude is that of group approval. The class must be challenged to want to improve their word usage, to set their own standards, and to help each other attain them. Some of the procedures described below will assist in forming such attitudes.

Remedial usage teaching. In a recent survey of English teaching which included hundreds of classroom observations, the writer noted a persistent laxity in checking and correcting the speech errors of pupils in ordinary classroom discussion and recitation. The following errors passed with no comment or correction of the teacher, even though the lessons were labeled "English."

Classroom Errors in English Usage

Pleonasm
Repeated subject: my
dog, he   49

Double negatives
don't have no, etc.   29
ain't got no   4
can't hardly (too fre-
quent to record)

Pronouns
them (them books, etc.)   11
this here (followed by
noun)   18
those there, that there   4
it don't   4
hisself, theirselves   2
what (the man what)   2
these kind   1
me and him (subject)   1
which (the man which)   1

Verbs, and agreement in
number
was for *were* (we was,
etc.)   16
lay for *lie* (lay down!)   12
come for *came* (he come
in)   11
is with plural (there's
four people here)   8
ain't for *isn't* (exclusive
of double negative)   6
seen for *saw*   5
says for *said*   3
tooken for *taken*   2

Verbs (*cont'd*)
are for *is* (another example are the Indians)   2
have broke   2
run for *ran*   2
leave or *left* for *let*   2
setting for *sitting*, *done*
for *did*, *risen* for
raised, *threw* for
thrown, has came,
have took, *raise* for
rise, *give* for *gave*,
I got (present
tense), was froze
(each item)   1
incorrect verb forms
chosed, b e n d e d,
growed, drownded,
stringed, l o s e d,
builded, s n u c k,
clumb, each item   1

Adjectives and abverbs
good for *well* (do it
good)   5
real good   3
lived simple   1
treat them rough   1
look careful   1
getting more foggier   1

Idiom
by (meaning to or at)   4
seems like, exciting like   4
this guy   1
different than   1
enduring for *during*   1

SUMMARY OF THE TABLE

Type of Error	No.	Per cent of total
Pleonasm	49	20
Double negative	33	14
Pronouns	44	18
Verbs and agreement......	94	39
Adjectives and adverbs....	12	5
Idiom	11	4
Totals	243	100

Certain theorists in recent years have argued that a child must never be interrupted to make a speech correction, for fear of destroying his train of thought, or confidence in himself. The uncritical acceptance of this theory has resulted in the kind of laxity noted above. Every parent knows that a child's speech can be corrected immediately hundreds of times without decreasing the child's power to communicate. The time to spare the child's feelings is *when he is the center of attention before a group.* Hence, the following practices are recommended: in conversation, ordinary discussion, and informal recitation, stop the pupil at once when he employs faulty usage of the serious (Outline I, page 218) type. Let him repeat his statement in the proper idiom. On the other hand, when he stands alone before a group to give a talk, tell a story, or make a report, allow him to finish uninterrupted, but before he is dismissed, require him to rephrase faulty expressions which the teacher has noted. Close attention to the principle of *no exceptions* to good usage will do much to raise the level of expression of a class.

Another sound principle in this connection is that speech-error corrections should be made by the teacher, rather than by pupils for two good reasons. One reason is that the attention of pupils should be centered on the content and effectiveness of their fellow-pupils' talks. Their criticisms should deal with organization, delivery, interest, and general success. The second reason is that pupils rarely have the discrimination to select the most important corrections; they tend to pick on minor or inconsequential items. In a class recently observed, a boy telling a personal experience wound up with the exclamation, "And was we mad!" The first correction offered was to change *mad* to *angry!* No one noticed or corrected the "was we."

In addition to classroom standards of good usage, it is possible to secure all-school agreement on certain fundamentals. A procedure frequently followed is for the English teacher or English department of a high school to draw up a list of minimum essentials for which all-school support is desired. The items of the list should be few, and they should be of the type having high frequency and high social penalty. When the English department is satisfied that the list represents the most important needs, it is presented to the faculty of the school for discussion. Voluntary acceptance of the list with the active support of all teachers is the goal. Naturally persuasion and some demonstration of the ultimate benefits of group action are superior tactics to administrative enforcement or accusations of past neglect.

High-school pupils, particularly those of the freshman and sophomore years, are stimulated by group decisions and are moved to action by having arrived at the answers to usage problems for themselves. For this reason it is important to get the group to join with the teacher in setting up standards of good usage for the classroom. The first step in the procedure is to set up goals which the pupils recognize as just and which are not too difficult of attainment. Standards of oral speech might be considered first, pupils and teachers talking over together certain minimum goals of achievement for the first months of the school year. These items can be listed on the blackboard, noted by the students in their notebooks, and a concerted effort made by the group to achieve some degree of success in overcoming the basic errors. The next stage is to take up certain items of incorrect usage which appear in their written composition. These should be discussed again with the group and a group agreement reached on those items which are important enough to demand class and individual attention. When these have been agreed upon, and have been recorded in their notebooks as items to study, from that time on particular attention should be given in all class work to see that the errors are corrected by the students in their written papers before the papers are handed in. The secret throughout this individualized and group action is to be sure that the pupils agree with the teacher on the importance of the corrections.

Very good attitudes can be formed, and good instruction given simultaneously, by setting the pupils specific problems in usage to solve for themselves. Part of the resistance of students to usage instruction is the fact that they are constantly being submitted to standards which to them seem artificial. They resist having to bow to rules for which at the moment they see no particular use. When usage problems arise in class, either as the result of a question raised by a pupil or from something appearing in a written paper, the teacher may assign to the class the task of finding out what good usage in that particular item is. Some students should be directed to newspapers, magazines, and other sources of printed material; some others may be assigned to listen to the speech of people who are reasonably acceptable as good speakers, and still others may be sent to reference works to look up the item and report back to the class their findings. After several days have been allowed for investigation, the class can hold a symposium on that particular item of usage and come to a decision about it. A decision reached in this way by the students from their own investigation will not only yield an answer which they are willing to accept as setting a standard, but it also creates an attitude in their minds of the way in which all usage items are to be resolved, and builds an attitude of good-will toward correctness. The spirit of group approval, arrived at by observation and investigation, is one which will go a long way to overcome the customary resistance to corrective teaching.

A carefully worked out technique of proof-reading can do a great deal to improve standards of written work and correctness in composition. For some reason it is very difficult to get students to reread their own work with a critical and corrective eye. The best procedure is one which is worked out with the group as a whole. When a set of compositions is ready to be handed in, the teacher should follow an accepted procedure of proof-reading. The first step is to check the title of the paper, to make sure that it is correctly placed on the paper, has capital letters where capitals are required, and that it is correctly punctuated. The next step is to scan the paper for paragraph form. Each paragraph should be properly indented; the first sentence in the paragraph should naturally begin with a capital letter; and there should be some kind of break in the composition to show the changes of thought. The next stage is to check the whole paper for accuracy in spelling and then for accuracy in word usage. Pupils that are dubious of the acceptability of certain phrases, or are unsure of the idiom they have employed should ask the help of the teacher before handing in the paper. In some cases it may be advisable to have the papers read over by a fellow-student after the writer has made his corrections as a kind of double check on the accuracy. This careful proof-reading if followed without fail at the time each paper is to be handed in will have a vigorous effect, first in getting pupils to give their own papers a correction before they are handed in and an attitude of respect for correctness and accuracy in all work. In all but exceptional cases, pupils will meet standards which are clear, attainable, and undeviatingly demanded. Much of the carelessness and inaccuracy of high-school written work is attributable to the relaxation of standards, not only in non-English classrooms, but even the English classrooms themselves. A custom of guided proof-reading to precede the handing in of papers will go a long way to reduce carelessness and inaccuracy of usage.

Still another remedial procedure is the keeping of cumulative error record cards. At the time the first composition is returned to the pupils, with errors noted by underlining or marks in the margins, each pupil is given a blank 5 x 8 filing card. At the top he writes his name and any other information the teacher may desire. He then makes a record on the card of the errors which appear on his composition, particularly those related to accuracy of usage. This recording serves a double purpose. It centers the pupil's attention on the errors he has made, and it also gives him a memorandum of what to avoid in his next writing. When the errors on the first composition have been listed on the card, the cards are collected by the teacher and kept in a file. Each time a

new composition is returned, the cards are returned at
the same time for a new listing of errors. By the use of
the card, the pupil sees pointedly the kinds of errors
which he is prone to make, discovers the errors of past
papers which he has now overcome, and he sees any
new errors which have arisen on the last paper. From
these notations each pupil may form his own goals of
matters demanding first importance in all his written
work. The teacher, by filing the cards, has a record of
the pupils' progress toward correctness, and a specific
source of information in conferring with pupils and
parents, and in grading pupils' work.

Nearly all remedial work in usage at the high-school
level is of an individual character. Very seldom is an
entire class in need of corrective teaching. Consequently,
the corrective instruction should be individualized as
much as possible. Some teachers meet this need by the
preparation of usage practice sheets. Take for example
the common confusion of *good* and *well*. The sheet is
headed "Adjective-adverb: good, well." A short explanation of the uses of the adjective and adverb appears at
the top of the sheet. Then follows a long list of exercise
sentences to give practice in the correct use of *good* and
well. A separate sheet of this kind is made for each type
of usage error frequent enough to call for corrective aid.
The sheets are kept in an indexed file accessible to the
pupils. When a pupil commits a certain error on which
he seems to need instruction and drill, he is directed to
go to the file, find the sheet he needs, and perform the
exercise, handing it in for correction when he is finished.
Through the use of such a file the pupil gets the specific
help he needs, he gets it at the time he feels the need,
and is therefore most ready to profit from the instruction, and the teacher is left free to work with the class

on other matters. Also important is the fact that proficient pupils who need no correction are not subjected to the tiresome process of listening to, or participating in, unnecessary corrective instruction. It takes some considerable time to prepare the sheets in the first place, but when the sheet is made and the stencil cut, it can be used for years, the stock replenished by running off a new supply from the stencil. In large schools committees of teachers can prepare the sheets, thus reducing the task for each individual teacher.

Creative language teaching. Teaching good usage creatively is identical with the art of teaching pupils to communicate. While the illustrations given here are drawn from written composition, the principles of language development apply with equal force to oral communication. The power to communicate effectively and correctly is advanced as the pupil makes progress in two areas: (1) an ever increasing knowledge of his total environment through active living, absorbing experiences, developing new interests and relating each new specific gain to the total body of his knowledge; (2) an increasing command of words, word-groups, and sentence patterns to facilitate the expression and interpretation of his experiences. Teaching the pupil thus to communicate is the art of composition, and composition is here defined as the personal expression of a person who has something to communicate, and has also the desire to make his communication influence others.

Under this definition certain high-school exercises cannot properly be classed as composition. The writing of summaries, digests, and précis of books and articles is a valuable exercise in thinking and organizing, as well as an aid to effective reading, but since the communication does not originate with the pupil, the activity is not composition. Writing paragraphs on assigned subjects, or to illustrate a type of writing, or to practice types of sentence structure are activities of instructional value, but they are frequently not composition in the sense of communication. Book reviews, written topics on factual subjects, and even thousand-word expositions may fail to become composition in the sense here intended, because the pupil has neither the need nor the first-hand experience to communicate for himself in the assigned or suggested subject.

It is possible for a pupil to go through high school and receive good grades in English without learning the difference between writing and communicating. A number of them reach fourth-year high-school English. They write neat and often mechanically perfect papers with one, two, or three paragraphs arranged in proper sequence. But the subject and its treatment are entirely second-hand. The pupil has absorbed from reading or listening certain facts or ideas which he repeats more or less in his own words with a glib facility. The subject has no real significance to him, nor has it raised any internal response. His product contains nothing which he himself has said. In the process of writing he has been not much more than a kind of automatic relay between the source and the product. That there is a great deal of the so-called composition accepted in high schools is well known; that it is accepted because the concept of communication is not clearly recognized is the point of this discussion.

The requirements of a good composition are, first that the subject arise from a genuine need or interest of the pupil which stimulates him to thought and feeling; second, that he find for himself (with help if needed) the form or plan of the writing to develop it in his own way; and third, that when finished he has the sense of having made a statement, proclaimed an idea, defended a position, or expressed experience and feeling in prose or verse which is his own, and in which he can take pride. When these conditions are met in any piece of writing, that writing is truly composition, and is genuine communication.

In this source of motivation the urge to write is created internally. No subject is assigned, no set pattern is exacted, no uniform product is expected. The teacher of composition is not, except for routine exercises, a taskmaster. He is, instead, a self-starter, a spark-plug, a percussion-cap, or any figure of speech you like to indicate the one who sets off a train of action in another. Composition aroused in these ways can be real communication, and will be if the product is properly evaluated by class and teacher.

Honest and painstaking evaluation is as important to the development of true communication and correctness in writing as is the original motivation. No one expresses himself to a vacuum; very few write for themselves alone. We want recognition and appreciation. Very young children are satisfied with the response of a parent or teacher, but as we grow older we want the acclaim of our peers. Even the meetings of learned societies are half in the interest of learning in the abstract, and at least half to provide an audience for the writers of papers. To evaluate composition effectively, therefore, we must teach groups of pupils to listen with attention and courtesy, to judge fairly, to express opinions frankly but with due regard for the feelings of the author, and to appraise writing on its worth as communication. So to train a class as an audience is not easy, and cannot be done by a short lecture or a list of directions on the blackboard. It will take time, patient explanation of what is wanted, and most of all, a continuously good example in the teacher's own oral evaluations. But once established the virtue of such an audience in promoting honest, personal communication is ample reward for the effort.

Of equal importance are the evaluations which teachers place on papers. These are not merely grades, or corrections of errors. They should represent appraisal, or the measurement of the intrinsic worth of the writing. Such measurement means judgment in three factors: (1) A recognition of what the pupil sets out to do. This will differ for every paper and cannot be taken for granted. Indeed, one of the serious faults in evaluating composition is the confusing of what we think a pupil ought to do with a subject with what *he* intended to do. So far as in us lies, we must see the project as the author intended. (2) An appreciation of the plan the pupil adopted to carry out his idea. This means appraisal of the title and organization of the paper, a recognition of the balance of parts, and a sense of the appropriateness of form and language to the expression of his idea. (3) An evaluation of the success of the communication in terms of what the pupil set out to do. This judgment comes from a recognition of the clarity of ideas, the sequence of thought, the vividness of illustrations, figures, and conversation, and the sense of completeness of the whole. When the paper has been judged by these three factors, the pupil is entitled to a statement of appraisal, either orally in a conference, or as a written note on the paper.

So far nothing has been said about errors. There will be errors, of course. There are often errors of English in papers written by experienced teachers in summer-session courses. The fundamental attitude to take is that the errors are not sins in themselves, but are hindrances to the effectiveness of the communication. Every time the reader or a listener is confused, irritated, or amused by an error, the effectiveness of the communication is weakened to some degree. Byron found an easy rime by ending a stanza with the phrase, "There let him lay," but how many thousands of readers has he irritated or amused by his indifference to grammar! The sin is not in the word itself but in the effect it has on the reader's appreciation of the stanza in which it appears.

Since pupils are immature, careless, and imitative of the language they hear, their papers will have errors of sentence structure, of grammar, of idiom and usage, of mechanics of writing, and of spelling. There are deficiencies in the use of language as the medium of communication which can and must be corrected. The remedial procedures are discussed above. But in creative teaching the emphasis must be on the communication and not on the errors. When the pupil has something to say, when he wants to say it as well as he can, and when he appreciates the applause and criticisms of his fellows and of his teacher, the correction of errors as impediments to the success of his project makes sense and enlists his personal desire for improvement. On the other hand, decades of experience have proved that the correction of errors as errors, and drill on corrective measures in isolation from the need to communicate, result in discouraging returns from the time and effort expended. It cannot be claimed that attention to communication will eliminate errors. It is possible, however, staunchly to defend the position that emphasis on communication will subordinate the correction of errors to an element of the

total success, and that this emphasis will provide a genuine motivation toward accuracy and exactness never
aroused by red ink, failing grades, or isolated usage
drills.

Finally, the plea of this section is that the time given to
formal drill and grammatical analysis be transferred to
the promotion of good communication. Writing should
be frequent and as far as possible voluntary. Much time
should be devoted to the hearing and evaluating of writing. Compositions should be posted, with frequent
changes of display. And the teaching of usage and correctness should feature creative language situations: how
should a certain idea be expressed before a certain
audience; what effect do certain phrases have on the
intent and tone of communication; how would two people of differing age, social status, or degree of education
tell the same story or relate the same event; how would
one phrase a story or conversation to show the person-
ality of the speaker; and many similar situations. This
positive handling of language will stimulate creative expression, will reveal the relative nature of usage rules
and prescriptions, and will provide the ground for the
consideration of usage and idiom as they affect communication. And of great importance, the pupil's attitude
will shift from the discouragement of being found always in the wrong to the enthusiasm of experimenting
with language, all kinds of language, to discover what
he can do with it.

XII

The Evaluation of Usage Teaching

Ideally the evaluation of instruction in usage is to be found in the improved speech and composition of pupils in each class. This kind of evaluation, while gratifying in the long run to the teacher who can perceive the gradual disappearance of major faults and an increase in the use of desirable patterns, is too slow, too individual, and too subjective to serve as the measure of success of the teacher or progress of the pupils. It is necessary, therefore, to devise methods of sampling usage habits and skills at intervals in the pupils' progress in order to encourage them to greater effort by a recognition of what they have already accomplished. It is equally necessary for the teacher to find out from time to time how successful the instruction has been, where certain elements need strengthening, and where others may be dropped because the need for them has disappeared. This chapter will offer a discussion of the types of usage tests for various purposes, with samples of tests at various levels and suggestions for the making of usage tests.

DIAGNOSIS OF PUPIL DIFFICULTY

Since all instruction in usage should be based upon the major needs of the pupils in each class, it is important at the outset to discover what these needs are. Tests for this purpose are called *diagnostic* tests, and are constructed to reveal for each individual pupil the number and kinds of faulty usages and undesirable language habits which are characteristic of his speech and writing. The teacher who possesses this information can plan class activities which will meet the needs of the greatest number of pupils, and can give particular help to pupils having exceptional or peculiar difficulties. Diagnostic analysis can be made of spoken English and of written English.

Diagnosis of speech errors. Procedures in the diagnosis of speech errors are fundamentally the same at all levels. The steps are: (1) The preparation of a chart containing the most characteristic and least desirable speech forms of the particular grade level. Usage list A or I in Chapters IX, X, and XI will provide the information needed to form such a chart for the elementary grades, the junior high school, and the senior high school. (2) The planning of class activities such as discussions, panels, and brief speeches which will provide opportunities for pupils to use their natural speech. (3) The conscientious recording by the teacher on the chart the speech errors of each pupil. There should be at least three observations of each pupil's speech habits. (4) Analysis of the chart to discover the most persistent difficulties of the class as a whole, and the chief difficulties of each pupil. (5) Instructional procedures to attack and eliminate the principal faults.

The following sample is a chart prepared for the lowest grades of the elementary school. The same form can be used to prepare a chart for any grade level, the items to be selected from the appropriate list in Chapters IX, X, and XI.

ANALYSIS OF PUPIL ERRORS IN ENGLISH USAGE IN NATURAL
SPEECH: KINDERGARTEN AND GRADES ONE THROUGH THREE

	John	Mary	Tom	Jean
Pronouns				
1. My brother, *he*, etc.				
2. *her, him, me*, as subjects				
3. *hisself, theirselves*				
4. *them* for *those*				
5. *This here, that there*				
6. *us* girls, boys, etc. as subjects				
7. with *we* boys				
8. *yourn, hern, ourn, theirn*				
9.				
Verbs				
1. *ain't* for *isn't* or *am not*				
2. have *ate*				
3. was *broke* (broken)				
4. he, she *come*				
5. have *did*				
6. he, she, it *don't*				
7. he *give*				
8. *knowed, growed, throwed*, etc.				
9. I, he, she *says* (past tense)				
10. I, he *seen*				
11. have *saw*				
12. we, you, they *was*				
13. have *went*				
14.				
Negatives				
1. I *ain't got no*				
2. *don't have no*				
3. *didn't do nothing*				
Miscellaneous				
1. *a* orange				
2. would *of* for *have*				
3.				

Diagnosis of errors in writing. There are two methods to employ in determining the characteristic usage errors in writing of a class or individual. The first method is the analysis of the written work of a class from compositions, letters, written exercises, and subject-matter examinations. The procedure in this case is essentially the same as for the analysis of speech errors. Having formed a chart of the significant usage errors for any particular grade level, the teacher then takes a sampling of written work of each pupil and enters on the chart the errors which appear on the papers. Pupils in the senior high school can profitably make such an analysis themselves. Provide them with a mimeographed chart of basic errors and several samples of their own writing which have been corrected by the teachers. As they enter the items on the chart, they can see graphically the errors which are constant and persistent as well as those which are accidental or the result of momentary carelessness. Repetitions of this analysis at intervals of a month or so will provide visible evidence of improvement, and will serve to motivate conscious efforts toward the elimination of basic faults.

The second method to determine usage faults in written English is to devise a test to be administered to pupils to sample their usage habits. Such tests have been used for many years, but they have frequently contained two faults. One fault is the tendency to overload the test with specific items—in other words, to present too many matters at one time. The second fault is a lack of discrimination in the *importance* of the items included. Instead of limiting the tests to items of great frequency and acknowledged undesirability, the tests have included disputed usages, unusual constructions, and in some cases fully acceptable usage.

The following sample is a diagnostic test designed for the junior high-school grades. It includes only items of prime importance at this level, and presents the usage elements in language situations as close to normal communication as an artificial test can get.

This test requires the pupil to rewrite those sentences which he feels are expressed in undesirable patterns. This procedure is more time-consuming than that of crossing out alternate forms or filling in blanks, but it has the virtue of requiring the pupil to think for himself the proper usage form, and to reinforce his decision by actually writing it out. In tests of alternate forms ("My sister has *broke, broken* her doll") the decision is made as a choice between two *words* more or less in isolation; the pupil does not have to think through the usage pattern as a complete communication.

DIAGNOSTIC TEST OF WORD-USAGE
GRADES SEVEN AND EIGHT

DIRECTIONS: Read each sentence carefully. Many of these sentences contain errors of word usage. After each sentence which you feel is incorrectly expressed, place a large X. When you have marked all the incorrect sentences in this way, rewrite each sentence you have marked so that it is expressed in correct English. Write your corrections neatly and clearly.

1. Jim and me was chosen to pick the teams.
2. The crowd cheered for John and I.
3. Daddy, please take Mary and I to the movies.
4. No one had ever seen them before.
5. Why won't you let we boys swim today?
6. That's the teacher which we boys like best.
7. When the doctor came, he ask me to get some water.
8. One of these four boys is guilty of stealing.
9. Hurry up, the show has began!
10. The kitten has drunk all the milk.
11. I wish I hadn't broke my skates.

12. When everyone has came in, we stand and salute the flag.
13. Everyone thought that Alfred done the best.
14. I wish you would let me help you.
15. When all had drank their coffee, the party broke up.
16. When I was a child, my aunt always give me cookies and cakes.
17. Mother said she would let us girls have a dance on Friday night.
18. He run out into the street and was struck by the car.
19. Last night I seen a fine show at the Orpheum.
20. No one has went that way before.
21. One of the eleven football players were hurt in the first scrimmage.
22. Press lightly; it don't take much force.
23. This is a secret between Mary and me.
24. If there's two roads, take the one to the right.
25. We haven't any ice-cream today.
26. If I only had of come earlier!
27. Each player has chosen his partner.
28. I asked him to learn me to swim.
29. How can you leave him do such a thing?
30. There's something wrong with every one of them problems.
31. The photographer has taken a picture of each class.
32. I haven't never seen him before.
33. Why haven't you got no lunch today?
34. My uncle, he always takes us to baseball games.
35. Sometimes he takes John and me to the Ice Palace.

When this test is completed and scored, the teachers can easily prepare a chart of typical errors, placing at the top the item showing the greatest frequency of error, the next highest frequency record, and so on until each item is ranked according to difficulty for the particular class examined. This list will reveal three important kinds of information: (1) the usage errors common to the class or to large numbers; (2) the usage errors typical of certain pupils but not of the class; (3) the usage items which for this class cause no difficulty. After such diagnosis the teacher is ready to plan corrective teaching of the most direct and efficient type.

Similar diagnostic tests can be formed for any grade level, care being taken to select the items appropriate to the grade and of sufficient importance to justify the diagnostic procedure.

APPLICATION OF USAGE SKILLS

Following instruction in specific items of usage, or during the course of such instruction, it is important to apply the skills which have been taught to the normal speech and writing of pupils. Much of the fault to be found with usage teaching is the common procedure of teaching by means of textbook or work-book exercises which require the pupil to make choices in usage and grammar in sentences not of his own creation. These exercises are useful in the first stages of teaching and for guided practice during the learning period. But usage instruction must not stop at this point. It must be carried over immediately into the pupil's own use of language, for until he faces situations of usage choice in his own independent expression, he has not demonstrated his command of the correct forms.

Creative oral procedures. In the elementary school and to some extent in junior high school good usage patterns should be taught by ear. Children should be made conscious in usage instruction that they are hearing desirable patterns, and they should learn to listen to themselves and to their classmates to preserve the desirable patterns and to eliminate the undesirable ones. Following specific usage instruction these procedures may be used.

Questions and answer. One pupil is selected to ask

questions, which he addresses to the members of the class. The pupil called on is supposed to answer promptly and to follow the form of the question. For example, if the class has had instruction in the uses of *saw* and *seen,* the questioner might say, "Yesterday I saw a bluebird. Donald, have you seen a bluebird this year?" Donald could reply, "Yes, I saw one last week," or "No, I haven't seen one yet." While this exercise is a little artificial, it has the virtue of giving much practice in the hearing and using of correct patterns in sentences of the children's own making. This device is especially useful for practice in irregular verbs, in the construction of negatives ("Do you have a bicycle?" "No, I don't have one.") and in certain oral difficulties like *a apple,* and *hisself, theirselves.*

Story-telling. Incidents of personal experience which children like to tell provide good language practice. To illustrate: in connection with a birthday or Christmas several children may take turns telling what each gave or was given. The practice of the verb *give* would occur in sentences like, "I gave my mother a bottle of perfume; I gave my brother a pencil box. My mother gave me a sled," and so on for a number of statements.

Practice to avoid the double subject or pronoun can be provided by children's stories of episodes involving members of the family. A story about father would naturally present a number of situations in which "My father...." would begin the sentence. If teacher, speaker, and class are all on their toes to prevent the, "My father, he...." from appearing, these stories can provide excellent practice of the best sort.

Picture descriptions. Each child is encouraged to bring to school a picture, preferably colored and of good size, to show to the class. The child displaying the picture tells the story it presents. Following this members of the class ask questions about it. This exercise provides opportunities for a good deal of natural speech and can serve to practice forms of irregular verbs, of pronouns, and of subjects without the pleonastic pronoun (the dog, he....)

In the junior and senior high schools the same device can be used in the description of an object brought to class, in telling about a hobby, in demonstrating a process or a game at the blackboard, and so forth. The essential point is that the attention of the speaker and class is centered on the object or diagram; the speech patterns will be natural, and errors, if they occur, can be corrected in a setting of functional communication.

Creative written procedures. Immediately following a usage lesson, preferably in the same period, an assignment should be made to write a story or paragraph to apply the usage items which have been taught. While such writings are somewhat artificial, they serve to reinforce the instruction given and provide practice in the usage items in the pupil's own sentences.

To illustrate: a class having studied and practiced the case forms of personal pronouns in combinations (John and I, Henry and me, and so forth) might be assigned a story to write, the first sentence of which would be given by the teacher. The pupils would be asked to use the combination forms wherever applicable. Stories like this could be expected.

OUR PARTY

Since our birthdays are close together, mother said that John and I could have a party. We chose a date and sent out invitations. First we selected boys that both John and I knew. Then we each added two others to our list. On the day of the party everyone came. Each one brought gifts for John and me. We enjoyed opening the packages. After that we played games. John and I didn't play but acted as judges of each game. After the games we awarded the prizes which John and I had chosen. The party ended with refreshments and singing. All the guests had a good time and so did John and I.

Similar exercises can be assigned to practice groups of irregular verbs. The teacher can place on the blackboard any three or four verbs having conceivable relationships of meaning and assign to the class the writing of a story or incident making use of the verbs in their various forms. Some sample groups are:

> run, swim, freeze
> break, tear, burst
> come, begin, teach

With a little help pupils can be stimulated to write short narratives using the verbs in a fairly natural setting.

Obviously the value of these exercises will lie in securing pupil interest and effort to use the various forms as intelligently and correctly as possible. The papers when completed should be collected for corrections by the teachers, or they may be corrected by a committee of students who have shown competence in good usage. During the writing it is wise to supervise the work, and to give particular attention to those students who are likely to go astray in the usage forms.

MEASUREMENT OF TEACHING SUCCESS

The success of instruction in English usage is naturally discovered in the improvement which pupils make in their use of English idiom in speech and writing. Three methods of determining progress, or in some cases lack of progress, are discussed below.

Comparison of pupil performance in the use of English. The teacher who has made an analysis of the speech errors of pupils on a chart like that described above in this chapter may repeat the observations and record the findings on a similar chart at the end of a semester or year of instruction. A comparison of the two charts should yield a qualitative measure of the success of instruction. Specifically the comparison should reveal: (1) speech errors which have been entirely eliminated; (2) speech errors formerly common to the class which now appear in the language of only a few pupils; (3) specific gains in command of good usage made by each pupil; (4) the gains made by the entire class as shown by the number and kinds of errors on the first chart not found on the second.

In written composition a similar comparison can be made. In the case of younger pupils the teacher will have to make the charts since the children are not all able to observe and record accurately from their written work. High-school pupils can in most cases make their own charts from written composition, and are able to derive insight into their own usage difficulties from the exercise. In making the comparison between earlier and later written work these conditions should be observed: (1) the same number of papers which formed the basis for making the original chart should be used in making the second; (2) the compositions should be of recent date; (3) the compositions used for the second chart should be of approximately the same type and subject matter as those used for the first chart. Preferably in each case the types of writing should vary, including, perhaps, one narrative, one report or exposition, and one essay or discussion.

Repetition of inventory or diagnostic test. In classes in which a diagnostic test like those described above in this chapter has been administered at the beginning of the school year, the same test may be repeated at the close of a semester or school year as a measurement of teaching success. It was pointed out earlier that such tests have the disadvantage of presenting usage situations in somewhat artificial settings, but this defect is partially outweighed by the range of items which the test can offer and the specific character of the results. When the returns of the second test have been tabulated, a comparison with the results of the first test should show: (1) the quantitative gain in usage accuracy of the class; (2) the specific improvement of each pupil; (3) the items eliminated or nearly eliminated as a result of instruction; (4) the items which persist in causing difficulty. From such retesting and analysis the teacher can pass on valuable information regarding the pupils to the teacher who will have them next and can also revise or reinforce teaching procedures for the next group to meet weaknesses or lacks of emphasis in instruction revealed by the comparison of tests.

The warning should be repeated that the value of such testing is lost if the pupils are deliberately coached to prepare themselves for a usage test. Such tests are only significant when they reflect the *normal habits* of pupils formed in the natural uses of speech and writing. Correctness to pass a test is worthless; good usage in the normal needs of writing and speaking is the only worthy goal.

General tests of English ability. Throughout this book the word *usage* has been employed in a narrow sense, to mean the choice of words, phrases, idioms, and syntax in the expression of ideas in speech or writing. Usage, however, is commonly understood in a wider application where it represents not only word-choice and word order, but all the mechanics of writing such as punctuation, capitalization, abbreviation, paragraphing, and even spelling. Published tests of English skills frequently are called tests of English usage, by which designation the broader sense of usage is intended. Such tests are often used in cities, counties, or states as a measure of pupil progress or teaching success in English skills.

In general these tests of English skills measure what pupils have learned *about* English from textbooks. They do not and cannot measure the pupil's ability to use English effectively as a vehicle of communication. For this reason teachers should be aware of the limitations of such tests, and should use the scores from such tests with caution. There are two reasonably valid uses of tests covering the English skills.

1. To compare the success of a class, school, or city system with a nationally determined set of norms. This comparison will show degree of success in handling the items of which the test is composed; it does not show in any way whether or not the pupils use English more or less effectively than any other group.

2. To form pupils into groups or sections for special types of teaching. The tests will reveal those pupils who are deficient in *mechanical* skills and possibly in word usage. The information is sufficiently accurate to discriminate between the really competent and the thoroughly deficient. Pupils who fall at the middle of the range of scores cannot be so easily classified by such tests. Such pupils are frequently competent in English expression but have one or more specific skill deficiencies as in spelling, punctuation, or word usage. For pupils at the middle of the range of scores the information yielded by the test should be supplemented by further specific tests before they are arbitrarily grouped.

For a description and evaluation of various English tests the best reference is *The 1940 Mental Measurements Yearbook*, edited by Oscar K. Buros and published at Highland Park, New Jersey. This book is generally available at reference libraries and in the educational libraries of colleges and universities. Approximately thirty different tests of English skills are listed; nearly all are described and evaluated by reviewers. A few tests are listed below to indicate the kinds of materials which are available. These tests are, in the opinion of the writer and subject to the limitations discussed above, reasonably valid for the measurement of English skills for pupils in large groups.

LOWER ELEMENTARY GRADES

Since objective testing involves the skills of reading for meaning, following printed directions, and the writing of legible answers, it is obvious that formal, printed tests can be of little use below grade 3. Even in grades 3 and 4 it is not easy to determine whether lack of success in a usage test is owing to faulty language habits or to inability to read the test and write the answers. For this reason objective tests of language skills and usage are not recommended for the lower grades of the elementary school.

UPPER ELEMENTARY GRADES

PRESSEY, S. L., and others, *English Tests for Grades 5 to 8* (Bloomington, Ill., Public School Publishing Company, 1938).

These are diagnostic tests of pupil skills in capitalization, punctuation, word usage, and sentence structure. Three forms are available; the tests are simple to administer and easy to score. A diagnostic record chart is provided for analyzing the needs of classes and individual pupils.

JUNIOR HIGH SCHOOL GRADES

SMITH, Dora V., and McCULLOUGH, Constance, *Essentials of English Tests* (Minneapolis, Minn., Educational Test Bureau, Inc., 1940).

These tests are designed to measure general English skills for grades 7 through 13. They are easy to administer and easy to score, except for the last part which requires close discrimination of a large number of items. This difficulty is compensated for in the validity of the content of the test, which is of a high order. Two forms are available.

Senior High School Grades

In addition to *Essentials of English Tests* described above, the following will be found useful:

Coöperative Test Service, *Effectiveness of Expression Tests,* Coöperative English Tests (New York, Coöperative Test Service, 1945).

Prepared by a large number of experienced teachers, these tests attempt with reasonable success to measure more than mechanics and form. In addition to basic English skills they test skill in sentence formation, paragraph recognition, and organization of writing.

Cross, E. A., *Cross English Test* (Yonkers-on-Hudson, N. Y., World Book Company, 1923).

One of the older tests, in continuous use since 1923, this one measures skill in pronunciation, sentence recognition, spelling, punctuation, and word usage. Three forms are available. Some of the parts are too brief to be accurately diagnostic, but the test as a whole yields a composite score sufficiently reliable for the comparison of classes or groups or the placement of pupils into sections. It is easy to administer and to score.

A SELECTED BIBLIOGRAPHY

This list is composed principally of books and articles consulted in the preparation of this work. For reference to fuller bibliography, see footnote 1, page 35.

※   ※   ※   ※   ※   ※

ALFORD, Henry, *A Plea for the Queen's English* (New York, 1872).

BEVIER, Thyra Jane, "American Use of the Subjunctive," *American Speech,* Vol. 6 (February, 1931), p. 207.

BRIDGES, Robert, "On English Homophones," London, Society for Pure English, Tract II, 1919.

BROOKS, Stratton D., *English Composition* (New York, American Book Company, 1911), Book I.

BROWN, Goold, *Grammar of English Grammars* (New York, 1851).

———, *The Institutes of English Grammar* (Second Edition, New York, 1825).

BRYAN, W. F., "Notes on the Founders of Prescriptive Grammar," Manley Anniversary Studies in English Literature (Chicago, University of Chicago Press, 1923).

BRYANT, Margaret M., *A Functional English Grammar* (Boston, D. C. Heath and Company, 1945).

BULLION, Peter, *Principles of English Grammar* (New Edition, New York, 1844).

BURLINGTON RAILROAD, *Burlington Blues,* December 20, 1926.

CANBY, H. S., "Correctness," *The Saturday Review of Literature,* Vol. 5, p. 137.

CLIPPINGER, Merle E., *Written and Spoken English* (Boston, Silver, Burdett and Company, 1917).

CROSS, E. A., *Fundamentals in English* (New York, The Macmillan Company, 1926).

CURME, George O., "The Split Infinitive," *American Speech,* Vol. 2 (May, 1927).

———, *Syntax* (Boston, D. C. Heath and Company, 1931).

ELLIS, Havelock, *The Dance of Life* (Boston, Houghton Mifflin Company, 1923).

FOWLER, H. W., *A Dictionary of Modern English Usage* (Oxford, Clarendon Press, 1926).

FRENCH, John C., *Writing* (New York, Harcourt, Brace and Company, 1924).

FRENCH, N. R., CARTER, C. W., Jr., and KOENIG, Walter, *The Words and Sounds of Telephone Conversations*, Monograph B.-491 (New York, Bell Telephone System, June, 1930).

FRIES, Charles C., *American English Grammar*, English Monograph No. 10 of the National Council of Teachers of English (New York, D. Appleton-Century Company, Inc., 1940).

———, "The Expression of the Future," *Language*, Vol. 3, No. 2 (June, 1927).

———, "The Periphrastic Future with *Shall* and *Will* in Modern English," *PMLA*, Vol. 40, No. 4 (December, 1925).

———, "Rules of the Common School Grammars," *PMLA* (March, 1927).

———, *Teaching of the English Language* (New York, Thomas Nelson and Sons, 1927).

GREENE, Samuel S., *First Lessons in Grammar* (Philadelphia, 1848).

GREENOUGH, J. B., and KITTREDGE, G. L., *Words and Their Ways in English Speech* (New York, The Macmillan Company, 1922).

HALL, Fitzedward, *Modern English* (New York, 1873).

———, *Recent Exemplifications of False Philology* (New York, 1872).

HALL, J. Lesslie, *English Usage* (Chicago, Scott, Foresman and Company, 1917).

HODGSON, W. B., *Errors in the Use of English* (Edinburgh, 1889).

HYDE, Mary F., *Two-Book Course in English* (Boston, D. C. Heath and Company, 1900).

JESPERSEN, Otto, *Essentials of English Grammar* (New York, Henry Holt and Company, Inc., 1933).

———, *Growth and Structure of the English Language* (New York, D. Appleton-Century Company, Inc., 1929).

———, *Philosophy of Grammar* (New York, Henry Holt and Company, Inc., 1924).

KAULFERS, Walter V., *Four Studies in Teaching Grammar* (Stanford University, Calif., Stanford Bookstore, 1945).

KENNEDY, Arthur G., *Current English, A study of present-day usages and tendencies, including pronunciation, spelling, grammatical practice, word-coining, and the shifting of meaning* (Boston, Ginn and Company, 1935).

———, *English Usage* (New York, D. Appleton-Century Company, Inc., 1942).

KENYON, J. K., "The Dangling Participle Due," *American Speech*, Vol. 6 (October, 1930).

KIMBALL, Lillian G., *Kimball's Elementary English* (New York, American Book Company, 1911), Books I, II.

KIRBY, T. J., and CARPENTER, M. F., *Pupil Activity English Series* (New York, Harcourt, Brace and Company, 1930), Books VII, VIII.

KIRKHAM, Samuel, *English Grammar in Familiar Lectures* (Eleventh Edition, Rochester, N. Y., 1830).

KITTREDGE, G. L., and FARLEY, F. E., *Advanced English Grammar* (New York, 1913).

KNOTT, Thomas A., "Standard English and Incorrect English," *American Speech*, Vol. 9 (1934), pp. 83-89.

KRAPP, G. P., *Comprehensive Guide to Good English* (Chicago, Rand McNally & Company, 1927).

———, *The Knowledge of English* (New York, Henry Holt and Company, Inc., 1927).

———, *Modern English* (New York, Charles Scribner's Sons, 1909).

LAMBERT, Mildred E., "Solidary Modification: Modes of Predication," *American Speech*, Vol. 4 (October, 1928), p. 29.

LEONARD, Sterling A., *Current English Usage*, English Monograph No. 1 of the National Council of Teachers of English (Chicago, National Council of Teachers of English, 1932).

———, *Doctrine of Correctness in English Usage, 1700-1800*, University of Wisconsin Studies in Language and Literature, No. 25 (Madison, Wis., 1929).

———, "Educational Quackery," *The Saturday Review of Literature*, Vol. 5 (March 23, 1929).

———, "Shall and Will," *American Speech*, Vol. 4 (August, 1929), p. 497.

———, "Usage Notes," *American Speech*, Vol. 4, p. 252.

———, and MOFFETT, H. Y., "Levels in English Usage," *English Journal* (May, 1927).

LEWIS, W. D., and HOSIC, J. F., *Practical English for High Schools* (New York, American Book Company, 1916).

LIVINGSTON, Arthur, "The Myth of Good English," *Century Magazine* (August, 1925).

LOUNSBURY, T. R., *History of the English Language* (New York, 1879).

———, *Standard of Usage in English* (New York, Harper & Brothers, 1908).

LYMAN, R. L., "English Grammar in American Schools Before 1850," U.S. Office of Education Bulletin No. 12 (Washington, D. C., 1921).

McFADDEN, E. B., and FERGUSON, A. C., *Language Series* (Chicago, Rand McNally & Company, 1919), Book III.

McKnight, George H., "Conservatism in American Speech," *American Speech*, Vol. 1 (October, 1925), p. 12.

——, *English Words and Their Background* (New York, D. Appleton-Century Company, Inc., 1923).

——, *Modern English in the Making* (New York, D. Appleton-Century Company, Inc., 1928).

Marckwardt, Albert H., and Walcott, Fred G., *Facts About Current English Usage*, English Monograph No. 7 of the National Council of Teachers of English (New York, D. Appleton-Century Company, Inc., 1938).

Marsh, George P., *Lectures on the English Language*, 1859; (Fourth Edition, New York, 1874).

Mencken, H. L., *The American Language* (Fourth Edition, New York, Alfred A. Knopf, 1936).

Moon, George Washington, *The Dean's English* (London, 1865).

Murray, Lindley, *English Grammar Adapted to the Different Classes of Learners* (Third Edition, Albany, 1802); two-volume edition (New York, 1817).

Pearson, H. C., and Kirchwey, M. F., *New Essentials of English* (New York, American Book Company, 1928).

Perrin, Porter G., *An Index to English* (Chicago, Scott, Foresman and Company, 1939).

Pooley, Robert C., "Grammar and Usage in Textbooks on English," Bulletin No. 14, University of Wisconsin Bureau of Educational Research (Madison, Wis., 1933).

——, "Handbook of Current English Usage," *Colorado State Teachers College Bulletin* (Greeley, Colo., June, 1930).

——, "Linguistics and the Teaching of the English Language," in *Essays on the Teaching of English* (Cambridge, Mass., Harvard University Press, 1940).

——, Kibbe, Delia, and LaBrant, Lou, *Handbook of English for Boys and Girls* (Chicago, Scott, Foresman and Company, 1939).

Pound, Louise, "The Value of English Linguistics to the Teacher," *American Speech*, Vol. 1 (1925), pp. 101-106.

Priestly, J., *Rudiments of English Grammar* (London, 1768).

Raymond, C. H., *Essentials of English Composition* (New York, D. Appleton-Century Company, Inc., 1925).

Robertson, W. Graham, "Whistler, Sargent, and Others," *Harper's Magazine* (October, 1931).

Sapir, Edward, *Language* (New York, Harcourt, Brace and Company, 1921).

Scott, F. N., and Southworth, G. A., *Lessons in English* (Chicago, Benjamin H. Sanborn and Company, 1925), Books I, II.

SETZLER, E. B., "Is the Subjunctive Disappearing?" *Anglo-Saxon* (November, 1927).

SMITH, Logan Pearsall, "English Idioms," Society for Pure English, Tract No. XII, London, 1923.

SMITH, Roswell, *English Grammar on the Productive System* (Second Edition, Philadelphia, 1834).

STEINBACH, Reuben, "The Misrelated Construction," *American Speech*, Vol. 5, p. 181.

———, "On Usage in English," *American Speech*, Vol. 4, p. 161.

STORMZAND, Martin J., and O'SHEA, M. V., *How Much English Grammar?* (Baltimore, Warwick and York, 1924).

SVARTENGREN, P. Hilding, "Feminine Gender in Anglo-American," *American Speech*, Vol. 3 (December, 1927), p. 83.

THOMAS, J. M., MANCHESTER, F. A., and SCOTT, F. W., *Composition for College Students* (New York, The Macmillan Company, 1925).

THOMAS, Russell B., "Language Attitude," *English Journal* (September, 1930).

WEBSTER, Noah, *Philosophical and Practical Grammar* (New Haven, 1807).

WELLS, W. H., *The Elements of English Grammar* (Andover, 1848).

WHITE, R. G., *Words and Their Uses*, 1870 (New Edition, New York, 1872).

WHITNEY, W. D., *Essentials of English Grammar* (Boston, 1877).

———, *Language, and the Study of Language* (New York, 1867); Fifth Edition (New York, 1872).

WYLD, H. C., *English Philology in English Universities* (Oxford, 1921).

ZIEGLSCHMID, A. J. Friederich, "If for Whether," *American Speech*, Vol. 5, p. 50.

Index

This index contains only the words, phrases, and grammatical terms mentioned or dealt with from the point of view of usage. For an analysis of the chapters the reader is referred to the table of contents.